CONTI

INTRODUCTION

The evangelical world is embroiled in another theological battle! For the last several decades the issue has been the nature of Scripture--is it errant or inerrant? Unquestionably this is a serious debate as it has to do with the nature of the book we call our authority. Surely our view of the inspiration of the Bible will have something to do with the nature of the gospel we preach. Yet there are those who hold different views of the inspiration of Scripture who agree as to the nature of the gospel.

The issue now jolting the evangelical scene centers on the nature of the gospel itself, and interestingly enough, the main proponents of both sides of this debate hold to the inerrancy of the Scriptures.

The debate was potentially present with the book <u>Grace</u> by Lewis Sperry Chafer.[1] Some questioned the view presented in it, but it never became a point of contention to any great extent. The debate was brought to a slow simmer with the statements made by Charles Ryrie in his book <u>Balancing the Christian Life</u>.[2] In some minds and places the controversy boiled, but it never erupted onto the evangelical scene to create a consuming controversy or to produce extensive disunity or damage overall. But now the issue has exploded and is threatening to rip apart the evangelical unity in a serious and devastating manner.

The two chief proponents have become John MacArthur and Zane Hodges. For some time Dr. Hodges had been arguing his position in several works[3] which attained only limited distribution, while he was also having a considerable influence in the classroom. As John MacArthur continued to encounter this viewpoint and its influence in the churches, he wrote a book defining the gospel in almost opposite terms.[4] Following MacArthur's strong presentation of his convictions, both Ryrie and Hodges answered with books.[5] Without question Hodges' book is the strongest and most persuasive presentation of their viewpoint, making it clear that he is now the spokesman for that position.

Perhaps some feel the debate is much ado about nothing --semantics, or maybe the wrangling of overly-sensitive theologians, or maybe the pride of opportunists trying to advance their own popularity and ministry. But the two leading proponents are convinced that the debate is extremely serious and that the very nature of the gospel itself is at stake.

Without identifying all the issues at this point, it is enough and necessary to say that the debate centers on the relation of faith and salvation to the Lordship of Jesus Christ. MacArthur is convinced that true saving faith includes in it a submission to the Lordship of Christ. Thus we shall refer to his position as "Lordship salvation." Hodges, on the other hand, is convinced that true saving faith does not include a submission to the Lordship of Christ. Thus we shall refer to his position as "non-lordship salvation." Admittedly these terms are not fully expressive or definitive of the views they represent, and neither side is satisfied with the word which speaks of its conviction. However they are easy terms for the reader to remember and identify, and so we will use them regardless of their deficiencies and weaknesses.

According to Hodges the Lordship view or the position MacArthur argues in his book is anything but the true gospel.

> It is grace and faith versus a works-righteousness system which is very close to Roman Catholic theology.[6]

> It is "a radical re-writing of the gospel."[7]

> It is "one of the worst distortions of the Bible in our day."[8]

> It "clashes with the repeated statements" of the apostle John.[9]

> It has "turned the meaning of faith upside down."[10]

> It is "a theological Trojan horse."[11]

> It makes salvation a contract between God and man.[12]

It is as a theology "a complete disaster."[13]

It drives its adherents "into a psychological shadowland."[14]

It destroys the ground of assurance for believers.[15]

It is to have faith in the powerless words of man.[16]

It is to handle the Scripture in a manner which is "grotesque distortion."[17]

It has a resolute blindness which resists obvious conclusions.[18]

Its discussion of Scripture at points wanders off "into a wasteland of obscuring and confusion."[19]

It is akin to Pharisaism.[20]

It is "Satanic at its core," and it is "encouraged by the Enemy of souls."[21]

Its message and doctrine would be unrecognizable by the New Testament writers.[22]

It seeks to make Christians obey by challenging them to question their salvation.[23]

It is so in error that it cannot possibly give true assurance of salvation to the Christian in this life.[24]

On the other hand, according to MacArthur, the non-lordship view (the position expounded by Hodges) is equally dangerous and destructive to the nature of the gospel.

It exalts a faith which it destroys.[25]

It makes faith a bare assent to the facts of the gospel.[26]

It divorces the gospel from a transforming commitment to the living Christ.[27]

It will secure only false conversions.[28]

It is the greatest weakness of American evangelical Christianity today.[29]

It is a tragic error as it teaches that one can become a Christian without being a follower of the Lord Jesus Christ.[30]

It promises a false peace to those not truly in God's family.[31]

It warps and sometimes completely destroys the gospel.[32]

It is a matter of eternal consequence.[33]

It is a distinctly different view of salvation than the Biblical one.[34]

It produces a false evangelism.[35]

It offers a false hope.[36]

It offers a salvation from hell but not from the bondage of iniquity.[37]

It offers a cheap grace.[38]

It feeds the sinfulness of the human heart by giving the promise of eternal life without surrender to divine authority.[39]

It makes obedience optional in the Christian life.[40]

It offers a salvation which involves no spiritual commitment, no turning from sin, no change in lifestyle, and no commitment to the authority of Christ.[41]

It separates salvation and discipleship and applies every recorded invitation of Jesus to discipleship and not salvation.[42]

In light of the above statements, who can deny that the chief proponents of the debate consider the issue of Lordship versus non-lordship salvation a serious matter, even involving the very nature of the gospel itself.

But what exactly is each side saying in this debate? Is it necessary for all those interested in understanding the issues of the debate to read the two large books on the subject? Certainly that would be the best way to analyze the two sides of the controversy. But this writer wonders how many will do that; and even how many, if they were to do that, would have a clear and analytical understanding of the issues.

Therefore there is the need for a brief summary of the arguments in the controversy--a summary which even the layman can understand. Yet the reader should not expect this to be a discussion which remains neutral on this important issue. Though the comparative chapters will be presented in an objective fashion, final chapters of critique will close the discussion of the subject.

The controversy is important and every Christian of our day needs to be informed on the subject, and needs to take a stand in the controversy. Both authors noted above are correct in one thing concerning the controversy--the nature of the gospel is at stake.

PART ONE

A Presentation of the Two Sides

of the Controversy

CHAPTER 1

NON-LORDSHIP SALVATION

It is obvious that Zane Hodges has given much study and thought to the concept of non-lordship salvation as evidenced in the major book[1] he has produced on the subject. This work stands as the most comprehensive and systematized presentation on that theology thus far. He has exegeted the Biblical passages and analyzed the issues which are central and essential to the debate. He has dealt fully also with the texts and contexts of Scripture which his opponents use against his view. He has organized the whole into a logical package which is quite convincing when studied and understood in its entirety.

The purpose of this chapter is to seek to understand his position. What is he saying in the presenting and defending of his view? Our analysis of his thinking will be set forth by means of several clear principles. These principles are summary statements which reflect the content of the chapters of his book. This present writer wants it clearly understood that these principles are his own as he understands Hodges' position and not as stated by Hodges himself. Along with the principles there will be a discussion of each principle for clarification. Documentation is given so that the reader can check the analysis in the Hodges book for himself.

PRINCIPLE ONE: The way of salvation is simple--it is by faith alone.

The above statement sounds like one which every Bible-believing Christian would gladly embrace with rejoicing. After all, is that not the conviction of the Reformation principle of *sola fide*--faith alone? Hodges thinks so, but obviously not all agree with that conclusion in light of what he states further on the subject.

He argues that we must let faith mean faith and nothing else.[2] The English word faith must be allowed to function as a fully adequate equivalent to its Greek counterpart. It has no hidden meaning not found in the English word. As one follows this principle and allows faith to be faith and to mean nothing else except faith, one will see that such concepts as submission, repentance, fruit, and others which Lordship salvation adds are not there at all.

How does Hodges answer the charges by Lordship salvation that such a definition of faith preaches a "cheap grace?"[3] He argues that grace is never cheap when it speaks of the enormous price God paid for sin so that man could have salvation freely.

How does he answer the charge by Lordship salvation that such a definition of faith offers to sinners an "easy believism?" He counters that any other view is "hard believism" which obviously is not Biblical because it fills faith with false concepts.

How does he answer the charge by Lordship salvation that such a definition of faith amounts to "mental assent?" He maintains that the Bible says nothing concerning two kinds of faith, such as a mental faith versus a true faith. The only distinction stated in the Bible is between faith and unbelief. He rejects any division which would see various aspects of faith such as mental, emotional, and volitional. Though not explicitly clear in his meaning, he even states in this discussion that it is possible to believe against one's will.

Therefore Hodges' view of faith is clear! According to the Bible, it is "the inward conviction that what God says to us in the gospel is true."[4] That is the reality and definition of faith and nothing more. It contains no thought of submission to the content believed, but only an agreement that the content is true. Again, this for Hodges is faith and nothing more can be nor need be added to the definition.

If Hodges were asked if this concept of faith is Scriptural, he would refer to such passages as John 6:47, the entirety of John's gospel, I John 5:9-13, Romans 4:3, John 11:25-26, John 20:30-31, and others.

Thus Hodges' view is clear--salvation is absolutely free as one simply takes God at His word in the gospel. It is to believe the facts of the gospel.[5] It involves no submission, no repentance, no change in life-style as a result, and no fruit that will necessarily follow. To add these as part of salvation or even evidences of salvation is to leave the reformation principle of *sola fide*--faith alone.

PRINCIPLE TWO: Assurance of salvation is based on the promise of the gospel and not on works, fruit, or perseverance.

Hodges contends that God by His own power and will gives the miracle of the new birth (James 1:17).[6] It is brought forth by the word of truth--God's word in the gospel. This new birth comes simply to the one who is thirsty (Revelation 22:17).[7] When the Word works the miracle of the new birth, it also brings assurance to the heart of the one believing. The new birth and assurance are inseparable as the one cannot exist without the other. Furthermore, assurance cannot be gained in any other way except by faith and the new birth (John 5:54).[8] Thus if one has saving faith he will also have assurance because to question the certainty of eternal life is to question the certainty of the gospel message itself.[9]

If one were to ask if this assurance will always be with the believer, Hodges would answer in the negative. It is possible for a believer to doubt (example--John the Baptist) and where there is doubt, there is no assurance. Therefore assurance is only certain and absolute at the point of initial saving faith, though one should have assurance daily by trusting in the promises of God. If one has never possessed at one point in his life the assurance of eternal life, that one has never been saved, for he has never believed the gospel.[10]

To summarize: when one believes the message of the gospel there comes the miracle of the new birth and the undeniable certainty of salvation. And it is the simple presentation of a free gospel which produces the new birth

and assurance.[11] To add anything to an "absolutely free"
gospel, such as Lordship salvation does, will impede the
work of the new birth as well as the assurance of salvation.
In simple words, Lordship theology cannot produce the new
birth and salvation or assurance.[12]

**PRINCIPLE THREE: Saving faith is a one-time
    experience, but its effect in giving eternal life
    is forever.**

Using the Biblical account of the woman at the well in
John 4, Hodges argues for the simplicity of a one-timeness
of saving faith.[13] Jesus told her if she would drink once
(aorist tense), the water he gave her would spring up
continually (present tense) into everlasting life. Thus the
drinking (faith) may or may not go on, but that will not
hinder the effect of the water--it is lasting. This, says
Hodges, is not what Lordship salvation teaches, for that
view demands that the drinking (the believing) must go on
and on.[14] Hodges sees his view not only evidenced in but
also consistent with the nature of the new birth as it is a one-
time permanent event.[15] Therefore since the results of the
initial drink (faith) are permanent and final, then that drink
(faith) is sufficient and need not be continued to sustain the
eternal life received.[16] The faith should continue, but
whatever the case, the eternal life is not dependent on that
continuation because of the simplicity and singleness of
saving faith.[17]
    Bible verses which Hodges uses to support his position
besides John 4 include John 6:37, Luke 18:17, John 5:25,
John 3:14-15, and Genesis 15:6.

**PRINCIPLE FOUR: Salvation and discipleship
    are distinct, and should never be confused or
    mingled lest the gospel message be destroyed.**

Hodges would admit that Christ spoke often about discipleship and its cost. He would also acknowledge that with the realization of the cost of discipleship comes the necessity on the part of the would-be disciple to count the cost. Hodges agrees further that there is a cost in education and growth in the school of Christ, and that good works are involved in this aspect of growth and development. But he insists that all of this is a separate issue from salvation and must never be confused or mingled with it.[18] Discipleship is hard and costly, while salvation is free.[19]

The mistake which Lordship salvation makes is to unite these two, and thus their doctrinal confusion and error concerning the nature of saving faith.[20] This false understanding also gives an erroneous view of Christian experience as Lordship salvation expects an eternal life which comes full-grown rather than as a seed which needs growth and cultivation.[21] The Christian life, says Hodges, is a process of education and it is not automatic.[22]

Because Romans 8:13 indicates that the believer has the option of living according to the flesh or according to the Spirit, good works are not certain; and neither can they be the basis of the assurance of salvation.[23] Christian growth and discipleship should be the experience of the believer; and yes, before these can take place one must be willing to pay the price, but that is an entirely separate matter from salvation.[24]

PRINCIPLE FIVE: **It is possible for those who have experienced true saving faith to drop out and even apostatize, but this has nothing to do with the reality or the truth or falsity of their faith.**

As Hodges separates salvation completely from the matter of discipleship, he admits it is wise and necessary for the believer to think carefully about enrolling as a disciple of Christ, because the course is very difficult to complete.[25] But if one counts the cost after salvation, and then enrolls as a disciple, it may be that even then he will not finish the course.[26] He contends that the Bible gives clear warning about "dropping out" of the discipleship program (Hebrews 10:19-25).[27] He is convinced that these verses of Hebrews are written to real believers as a real warning of the possibility of failure.[28] He also refers to I Corinthians 9:24-27 and II Timothy 4:7-8 to support his conviction.[29]

From this basis one can understand why he argues further that perseverance is a necessity for success as a disciple, but it too has nothing to do with producing or proving one's salvation.[30] A true Christian can quit not only as a disciple but also as a Christian. Furthermore, though unregenerate people did enroll as Jesus' disciples and failed (Judas for example), that does not mean that everyone who fails as a disciple is lost and has never been saved.[31]

When speaking of the defection of disciples from the Lord Jesus in John 6, Hodges concludes that some of them probably were saved and some of them probably were not.[32] The saved and the unsaved both followed Christ as disciples, and both the saved and the unsaved failed as they left Him over His word concerning eating His flesh and drinking His blood. If one asks why Jesus allowed these unsaved to follow as disciples, Hodges calls it an act of love by Christ.[33] The conclusion of this has to be that a disciple might be unsaved, while a non-disciple might be saved.[34]

In another book Hodges argues a Christian can even apostatize, as he speaks of the "apostate Christian" when referring to Hebrews 6:4-8.[35] He does admit such a one would be under divine judgment of various kinds (lingering illness, the loss of a loved one, and even physical death). Yet such a one would not be under any possibility of eternal judgment.[36]

PRINCIPLE SIX: Losing and the possibility of defeat must be a reality for the believer or the battle is not real and the morale of the believer is crushed.

Hodges acknowledges in agreement with this principle that discipleship is a royal war between God and Satan.[37] Anyone familiar with Ephesians 6:12-13 must admit this.[38] And if it is a true war, the believer can be defeated, but even if one is defeated, this does not mean that he is unsaved or an unbeliever as Lordship salvation argues.[39] It simply means the battle is real with winners and losers.

If defeat means one is lost, will this not be a crushing blow to "troop morale?"[40] In the hour of defeat, instead of the believer being comforted and assured by the knowledge he belongs to God, which, it is hoped, would result in his pressing onward to victory, will he not instead be tempted to give up the battle thinking he is lost and therefore has no use in continuing the fight?[41] Besides, what kind of a soldier is it who fights the spiritual battle only to prove he is saved? Would not such an individual be no more than a mercenary soldier?[42]

Hodges rejects the possibility that the Christian army is to be made up of mercenaries who fight only to prove they are true believers.[43] Rather, he insists, that which motivates the Christian soldier to victory is the knowledge and assurance that he is a citizen of heaven. He is convinced that even Paul used this motivation and never questioned his readers' salvation (see especially I Corinthians).[44] He accuses Lordship salvation of believing that the fear of eternal judgment motivates more effectively than God's glorious grace.[45] He insists that the law can never motivate one to holiness--only grace can accomplish that.

Not only did Paul refuse to question the salvation of his hearers as a motivation to godly living, argues Hodges, but so did every other New Testament writer. He is convinced that no New Testament writer ever questions the salvation of his readers.[46] Therefore this refusal gives clear evidence that the warfare is fought only from the basis of an assurance of grace. Lordship salvation destroys this basis for victory as every defeat discourages the reality and presence of grace in one's life.[47]

**PRINCIPLE SEVEN: The believer has the choice
to produce or not produce Christian fruit in
his life, and the absence of such is not a sign
one is lost, neither can it be a test of salvation.**

In Hodges' understanding Christian maturity and
fruitfulness are not automatic in the believer's life, but rather
they must be built in one's life (II Peter 1:8).[48] In fact the
believer can be barren, according to Peter in this verse. It is
the individual Christian's choice whether he will bear fruit
and grow to maturity or whether he will remain unfruitful
and immature.[49]

On the other hand, Lordship salvation says that the lack
of fruit is the sign one is lost. Such a view is not Biblical,
for the Scripture says that fruitlessness is simply the
evidence a believer has stopped growing.[50] This is the
reason the Bible is full of warnings to the believer of the
danger of inactivity (see Titus 3:8; I Corinthians 15:58; and
Titus 3:14).[51]

If one objects to this conviction on the basis of James 2
(faith without works is dead), Hodges is ready with an
answer. James in this section does not speak of a true
saving faith versus a false faith which does not save. Rather
he compares two kinds of saving faith--a live one and a dead
one.[52] Because his readers are Christians, Hodges
maintains, he could not be speaking of the possibility of a
false faith. James must be speaking of a true saving faith
which is not active. It is termed a dead faith because of its
inactivity.[53]

In James 2:26 James illustrates his discussion by a body
which is dead as it does not have the life-giving spirit
present.[54] Hodges argues that if he saw a dead body as he
walked down a street, he would be positive of two things.
First, such a dead body was at one time alive; and second, it
is now dead because of the absence of a life-giving spirit.[55]
One thing he says he would never conclude is that the body
had never been alive.

Thus according to Hodges, the "dead faith" spoken of by
James in chapter 2 is one which was once alive, but which is

now called dead because it is inactive. It would be inaccurate to say it never had been alive or that it was never a true saving faith. If it was ever a true saving faith, then it cannot be dead in the sense of now being a non-saving faith because of the singleness of faith we have already seen to be his conviction.

We have seen that according to Hodges a true faith can exist without works, but it is a dead faith in the sense of being inactive. Therefore the presence or absence of works cannot be the test of salvation. The choice to produce or not produce works rests with the individual believer.[56]

PRINCIPLE EIGHT: Fellowship with Christ is based on abiding in Him, but the believer can also choose not to abide in Christ, wherewith he loses his fellowship. The lack of abiding has only to do with fellowship and is not to be a test of salvation nor the basis of one's assurance.

Christ desires to fellowship with His people, and He even calls them to Himself to that privilege, but the choice is up to them. He will not force fellowship upon them because love loses its value if it is not free.[57] But Lordship salvation fails to understand this because it argues that true salvation guarantees one will love Christ.[58] The Bible knows nothing of a guaranteed love, says Hodges. In fact, the Bible teaches that the capacity to love must be developed (II Peter 1:5).[59]

The believer who abides with Christ and therefore has fellowship will experience the love of both the Father and the Son.[60] Paul prayed for believers to have that kind of inner experience of Christ (Ephesians 3:16-17).[61] Christ stated that the test of one's love for Him was obedience to His words,[62] but He did not state that obedience was to be a test of salvation. Even His disciples forsook him at the hour of His death (Matthew 25:56), showing that our Lord did not assume they would inevitably bring forth fruit.[63]

Hodges refers to the metaphor of the vine and the branch in John 15, stating it speaks to us of discipleship. It demonstrates that discipleship and fruit-bearing are not automatic.[64] If the believer does not abide--and that is a real possibility according to the metaphor--it does not prove he possesses a false faith. It only indicates he is not living in fellowship with Christ.[65] Such a believer will also place himself in a precarious position of divine judgment or chastisement as pictured in the branches which were gathered and thrown into the fire when they withered.[66]

It is possible for the believer who does not abide for a period of time to be restored, as seen in the apostles of Christ. They were restored following their failure after Christ had risen from the dead.[67] But one must never forget that the believer makes the choices and whatever he chooses cannot be the test nor assurance of his salvation.[68] One could be a believer and not abide in Christ. That is his choice!

PRINCIPLE NINE: Repentance is not a condition or part of salvation, neither is it confined to the unsaved or to the time of one's salvation.

Hodges makes no denial that repentance is in the Scriptures. But he does differ in his interpretation of the term repentance from the common understanding and he also redistributes the usual time element of the term.

First he is adamant that faith alone is the condition of salvation and saving faith does not include the concept of repentance.[69] He points to some of the great verses of salvation, such as Acts 16:31, and notes there is not one word in this salvation passage about repentance. He chastises Lordship salvation teachers for finding the doctrine of repentance by implication only in such a passage.[70] There can be no compromise here if one wishes to keep the Biblical concept of *sola fide*.[71] To add repentance to saving faith is a movement toward Roman Catholic dogma as it is to make repentance a condition of salvation.[72]

If one wonders how Hodges handles the numerous Scripture challenges to repent, he answers by putting repentance completely outside the transaction of salvation. He states that "the call to faith represents the call to eternal salvation," while "the call to repentance is the call to enter into harmonious relations with God."[73] Repentance may precede salvation, as it did in the case of Cornelius, or it may follow salvation, but it in no way is to be considered as part of one's salvation.[74]

According to this conviction one can be saved without having repented. It is hoped, for Hodges, repentance will follow; but not necessarily so. On the other hand, one could repent and be in a harmonious relation with God and yet not have been saved. Again, it is hoped, salvation will follow; but again, not necessarily so.

The Scriptural support which Hodges musters, besides Acts 16:31, is the gospel of John.[75] This is the only Biblical book written with an evangelistic purpose, and therefore we should consider its gospel complete. The word repentance is not used once in this book.

What of Luke and his numerous references to repentance? Hodges declares that he is not denying the need of repentance, but only that it does not have to do with salvation. Repentance does have to do with sinners finding spiritual health or the restoration of fellowship with Christ.[76] Fellowship is based on repentance, while justification is based on faith alone.[77] The prodigal in Luke 16 repented when in the far country, and this act of repentance turned him in the direction of fellowship with God. Thus the prodigal did repent and God used it to bring him to salvation, but it was some days or hours before he was saved and it was not part of his salvation. The salvation he received is "absolutely free."[78] But God not only uses repentance to bring men to faith and salvation; He also uses other means, such as gratitude, thirst, fear, etc.[79] Thus Hodges puts these on the same level of importance as repentance.

He further insists that all references to repentance can be interpreted in this manner. For example, when Luke 13:3,5

commands men to repent or perish, Hodges says this does
not refer to perishing for eternity, but rather to physical
death. This reference was fulfilled in the national tragedy of
70 A.D. when Jerusalem was attacked by the Romans.[80]

Clearly repentance for Hodges is different from the usual
understanding of the term. Repentance has no part in
salvation. Rather it is the setting one in the direction of God
and it may come before salvation or after salvation or
perhaps even never. It is possible to have an unrepentant
saved believer or a repentant unsaved unbeliever, because
the call to repentance is a call to fellowship and harmony
with God, while the call to faith is the call to salvation.

**PRINCIPLE TEN: The concept of Lordship is not
a condition of salvation, but should follow the
experience of salvation by faith alone, and it
will bring many glorious results.**

Hodges acknowledges that the experience of a born-
again believer ought to include good works, discipleship,
fellowship, and even walking in submission to Christ's
lordship.[81] But these are not conditions of salvation. He
returns to Acts 16:31 as a key example of a salvation verse
which says nothing of any condition except faith as the basis
of salvation.[82] Then he accuses Lordship theology of totally
mishandling this text by reading the concept of lordship into
the phrase "Lord Jesus Christ."[83] Hodges says they find
lordship in the word "believe" in this passage. He says this
is a well-known linguistic fallacy called "illegitimate total
transfer;"[84] that is, an idea drawn out of other words, or out
of the general context, and wrongly read back into a
particular word as part of its meaning.

He further argues that it is impossible for an unsaved
sinner to possess the power to submit to the lordship of
Christ. Only a believer can do this.[85] But after salvation
one is able to and should submit to Christ's lordship. This
submission is not necessary to salvation, but it is necessary
to be able to manifest the eternal life given by faith alone.[86]

The result of such a submission to Christ's lordship is Godward--it brings glory to God. But it is also manward--it brings the believer friendship with Christ. It is also worldward--it presents a powerful drawing testimony to the world.[87]

Thus Hodges is convinced that the concept of lordship is not a condition of salvation, but it should follow salvation by faith alone, and as it does it brings many glorious benefits.

PRINCIPLE ELEVEN: To make Lordship or anything else besides faith a condition of salvation is prideful and is akin to Pharisaism.

Hodges has what may be his strongest words against the proponents of Lordship salvation in a section where he implies that their position equates with Pharisaism.[88] He is careful not to make the accusation directly, but there is little doubt as to his meaning.

He begins by noting man's tendency to think he is good as illustrated in the elder brother of Luke 15 or the Pharisee who went to the temple to pray in Luke 18:9. He notes that men such as these are in every age--those who see themselves as righteous and at the same time regard others as religiously inferior to themselves.[89] They give God all the credit for their righteousness (see Luke 18:11-12--"I thank you that I am not as other men").[90] They also take their righteousness as an evidence of their salvation, yet they have forgotten that no one is good but God.[91] Is he not thinking of the Lordship salvation men here?

In this chapter Hodges further discusses the rich young ruler who was confident of his morality, yet still lacked faith. It was not that he lacked submission to Christ's lordship.[92] It is faith this sinner needed and not a submission to the lordship of Christ. Such a supposed submission (a submission he thought he had which he did not really possess) would only make him more Pharisaical.

Hodges is then convinced that we must reject this modern spirit of Pharisaism (Lordship salvation), which not only sees itself as spiritually superior, but gives God credit for it and then makes it a test of salvation--just like the Pharisees of old.

SUMMARY AND CONCLUSION

In order to see all the principles of Hodges as we have stated them to summarize his position, it will be helpful to list them once again.

1. The way of salvation is simple--it is by faith alone.

2. The assurance of salvation is based on the promise of the gospel and not on works, fruit, or perseverance.

3. The faith which saves is a one-time experience, but its effect in giving eternal life is forever.

4. The call to salvation and the call to discipleship are distinct and should never be confused or mingled lest the gospel message be destroyed.

5. Those who possess true saving faith can drop out and even apostatize, but this has nothing to do with the truth or falsity of their faith.

6. The possibility of dropping out and of being defeated must be a reality for the believer or the battle is not real and the morale of the believer is crushed.

7. The believer has the choice to produce or not produce fruit in his life, but the absence of fruit is no sign he is lost, and neither can it be a test of salvation.

8. Fellowship with Christ is based on abiding in Him, and the believer can chose to abide or not abide. Lack of abiding has only to do with fellowship, which the believer loses if he fails to abide. Abiding and fellowship are not to be a test of salvation or the basis of assurance.

9. Repentance is not a condition of salvation, neither is it confined to the unsaved or the moment of one's conversion.

10. The concept of lordship is not a condition of salvation, but should follow the experience of salvation by faith alone, and it will bring many glorious results.

11. To make lordship or anything else besides faith a condition of salvation is prideful and is akin to Pharisaism.

CHAPTER 2

LORDSHIP SALVATION

As the "Lordship salvation" controversy simmered for several years, no major spokesman emerged on the evangelical scene to articulate the position in an impacting manner. Concern was expressed in articles and sermons for what was seen as a new and less-than-Biblical gospel and for the evangelism some thought it was producing, but still no major spokesman rose to speak against it.

All of that changed with the publication of John MacArthur's <u>The Gospel according to Jesus</u>. In that single volume MacArthur not only articulated the Lordship position, but he also triggered the shot which brought forth the most systematic presentation of the non-lordship position, the work by Zane Hodges which we have just summarized.

In this chapter we will seek to present in summary form the convictions of MacArthur as found in his book. Again, we will set forth his position in the form of principles we have formed in reading and analyzing his view. If this section is longer than the one covering the non-lordship view, it is only because the MacArthur book has more content than the Hodges book. They are about the same number of pages, but the Hodges book is larger print.

PRINCIPLE ONE: **The gospel preached by Jesus is a far-cry from the gospel preached by many today.**

This principle is something of a theme or summary statement of the entire MacArthur book. The gospel preached by Jesus was a call to discipleship and submissive obedience, while the call of many today is a weak and fuzzy thrust which urges only an outward decision or the saying of a prayer.[1] The call of Christ was to turn from sin and be liberated from sin, while the call today leaves men in sin allowing the decision to turn from sin as optional for a future time.[2] The call of Christ urged one to count the cost of following Him, while the call today says nothing of the cost but instead offers an easy believism.[3] The call of Christ included a call to yield to His lordship, while the call today is simply to believe the facts of the gospel.[4]

The gospel preached by many today offers a justification separated from the reality of a transforming regeneration and sanctification.[5]

The gospel preached by many today presents a false faith, actually an unbelief, because it does not include in its message the sovereign right of Christ as Lord.[6]

The gospel preached by many today presents grace as weak, having power to change a sinner's standing before God, but not his unrepentant character.[7]

The gospel preached by many today bypasses repentance, making it something optional rather than part of true saving faith.[8]

On the other hand, the gospel preached by Jesus turned many away rather than fostering a quick, shallow, or easy response.[9]

Clearly, according to these definitions and distinctions, there is a difference between the gospel MacArthur advocates be preached and the one proclaimed by many evangelicals today.

PRINCIPLE TWO: The gospel preached by Jesus called for nothing short of the transformation brought by regeneration or the new birth.

The new birth which brings man's transformation is not the work of man--it is the work of God. Without it man has no hope of eternal life.[10] This was the message Christ gave to Nicodemus in John 3. In telling him he lacked this transformation of the new birth, Christ was informing him that his religious works were not enough--he must be

transformed by the power of God. He was telling
Nicodemus that his saving confession of faith in Christ was
not enough--he must be transformed by the power of
Christ.[11] He was telling him that salvation is not possible
apart from a divinely empowered regeneration.

For MacArthur and the proponents of Lordship salvation
it is unthinkable that such a powerful transformation as the
new birth could leave one as the slave of self and sin and
without a repentant heart.

PRINCIPLE THREE: **The gospel preached by
Jesus resulted in men and women worshipping
Him, and therefore a true response to the gos-
pel includes a submissive worshipful heart.**

This principle is spelled out by MacArthur in his
discussion of the woman at the well.[12] Strangely enough,
this is the same passage Hodges uses to illustrate that the
gospel makes no moral demands on the sinner's life in the
way of repentance or a change of life.[13] MacArthur
maintains this passage is not given as a normative for
evangelism, yet still in the conversation the woman is called
upon by Christ to face her sin.[14] Even the concept of the
verb "drink" conveys the idea of commitment.[15] Finally,
Christ challenges her to worship Him.[16] He challenged her
to be a true worshipper. MacArthur contends here that
salvation results in worship.[17] Surely, he argues, this shows
the fallacy of the contention that Jesus was offering her
eternal life apart from commitment, because a call to worship
entails a clear call "to the deepest and most comprehensive
kind of spiritual submission."[18] One cannot worship apart
from submission because submission is the heart and core of
worship. Spiritual worship is not possible by one harboring
sin in his or her life.[19]

PRINCIPLE FOUR: The gospel preached by Jesus was a gospel that deals with sin--He came to forgive and deliver the sinner from his sins.

MacArthur argues that one of the great weaknesses of modern evangelism is that it does not face men with the reality of their sin.[20] Any evangelistic message or method which bypasses sin is not the message or method of Christ, especially in light of the fact that sin is the real issue of salvation.[21] Christ came to forgive and deliver from the power of sin. Furthermore, His call to salvation goes out to sinners; not the righteous, but sinners who have come to recognize their sin and their unworthiness, and those who long to be forgiven and delivered from it.[22] Therefore, only when one has come to recognize his sin and the need of salvation, which includes forgiveness and deliverance from sin, will that one be a candidate for salvation.

The other side of the coin of truth is that Christ rejects the righteous; those who are convinced they are good enough; those who do not understand the serious nature of sin.[23] Any gospel which offers a salvation which does not face sin and its reality and the fact that in salvation Christ forgives and delivers from its enslavement is no gospel at all. Jesus came to save sinners!

PRINCIPLE FIVE: The gospel which Jesus preached called for more than an intellectual assent to certain facts, but it involved a divine miracle which opened blind spiritual eyes and gave a new heart.

Lordship salvation, says MacArthur, often is accused of trying to make theologians out of its evangelistic prospects in the presentation of the gospel.[24] MacArthur denies this accusation. He counterattacks by saying that to deny the reality of Christ's lordship in the salvation experience is to reduce salvation to mere intellectual assent to a certain set of Biblical facts.[25] If obedience, submission, and lordship are excluded, then all that is left in the gospel message is agreement with certain facts about Christ and salvation.

That no one is saved by simply knowing and believing the facts of the gospel is clearly illustrated in the healing of the blind man in John 9. The physical miracle did not bring him salvation. In the events which followed this miracle of healing, his understanding moved from recognition of Christ as "the man called Jesus" to "a prophet" to "Lord, I believe," followed by the worship of Christ (verse 38). Following the removal of the scales from his spiritual eyes, he saw Christ clearly for who He was and the certain response was worship.[26] Clearly the result of the miracle of spiritual sight was a surrendered, worshipping heart.[27] Though this miracle of spiritual sight stopped short of making the man a theologian, it was more than mere intellectual assent to the truth of Christ and the gospel.

PRINCIPLE SIX: The gospel preached by Jesus included the proclamation of the law so men would understand their sin and the necessity of turning from it as they turned to Christ in faith.

MacArthur notes that it is easy to get professions of faith in ministry today, but few of them follow through with any commitment in the modern church.[28] Something must be wrong with such an evangelistic method that produces so many failures.

Using the account of the rich young ruler, MacArthur seeks to point out such weakness in our present methods.[29] This young possessor of great wealth was correct in several areas. He had the right motive as he came seeking eternal life. He had the right attitude as he came humbly with a deep need. He came to the right source. He asked the right question. But his problem was a lack of the sense of sin. He was convinced that he had kept the commandments from his birth.

MacArthur notes that modern evangelism which centers on man's psychological needs may well have hustled him into a decision. After all, he sensed a need; he was anxious, lacking peace and joy. Maybe he was even desperate. But he had no sense of sin because he lacked an understanding of the law of God. Scriptural evangelism must bring a man face to face with himself and his sin by the perfect law of God. Christ would not receive him on his own terms. He must be brought to the place where he recognized his sin!

To show him his sin Christ challenged his claim to have kept the law by telling him he must sell his possessions, give the funds to the poor, and come follow Him. If the young man was really a keeper of the law, he would have no trouble with this, for one who loves his neighbor as himself would respond eagerly without any problem. When he was unwilling to do this, it should have shown him his sin!

But he failed the test. He could not see his sin. He wanted eternal life but without admitting and confessing his sin, and without surrendering to Christ. Christ refused to change the terms of salvation.

Surely the evangelistic method of Christ must be ours. Where there is a lack of a sense of sin, the law must be proclaimed so men will understand their sin and the necessity to turn from it in faith to surrender to Christ.

PRINCIPLE SEVEN: The gospel preached by Jesus radically changed men and their actions following an encounter with Him, and such an experience left no doubt about the reality of their salvation.

In a discussion of Luke 19 MacArthur uses Zaccheus as an example of this principle.[30] This despised outcast tax collector wanted to see Jesus. When he did his life was changed. That change is evidenced by his willingness to give half his possessions to the poor, and the further willingness to give back four times as much as he may have extracted from anyone by fraud. Christ's response was to assure him that on this day salvation had come to his house, because he too was a son of Abraham.

MacArthur sees in these words the evidence of a transformed man which in turn is the evidence of a true believer. Zaccheus did not accept the gift while rejecting the Giver and His authority over him. He did not debate or question the demands He made on his life.[31] This is the attitude and response one will find in the heart of every new believer--the desire to obey. True, Zaccheus was saved by faith, but the works which followed are an important evidence his faith was genuine.

Surely the gospel we preach also can be expected to change men and their actions, leaving no doubt of the possession of salvation.

PRINCIPLE EIGHT: **The gospel preached by Jesus at times encountered hardened hearts which professed faith in Him, but which proved later by their lives that they were not true believers.**

MacArthur's example here is Judas.[32] First, he professed faith in Christ. He also walked in close association with Him. Everyone must have thought he was a follower of the Lord Jesus. But he was a hypocrite, and Jesus knew it all the time (John 13:18). It's not that Judas was saved and then lost his salvation, for true salvation is eternal. It is that he was never truly saved. He stands as a continual warning concerning the possibility of being a casual and false professor.

Definitely a true believer can fail, but that is not the case of Judas. The other apostles failed, but they returned for forgiveness and cleansing. The true believer will never fall away completely, because saving faith is dynamic and transforming. Judas never was saved--he was a hypocrite who eventually showed his true colors.

We too can expect as we preach the gospel that at times we will encounter hardened hearts which will make false professions of faith. In time these lives will prove the falsity of their professions. Multitudes of such Judases may very well infest the churches of today.

PRINCIPLE NINE: The gospel preached by Jesus rested on the sovereign will of God and the faithful preaching of a saving faith which included humility, revelation, repentance, faith and submission.

The basis of argumentation at this point for MacArthur is Matthew 11:25-30, a passage he considers an invitation to salvation. He states that our Lord taught here that God Himself is "the determinative factor in salvation."[33] The preacher or witness is not responsible for the results, but only for an accurate and clear presentation of the gospel.

Along with this emphasis on the sovereignty of God in salvation in this passage, MacArthur sees five essential elements of saving faith.

1. Humility
   This passage states that the truth is hidden from the wise and prudent.[34] That is, human intellect cannot understand or receive spiritual truth. Therefore those who rely on their own wisdom and intellect are shut out.[35] Saving faith has a humility about it that depends upon God.

2. Revelation
   The truth of God is revealed to babes. Humility brings an understanding of God's revelation, while pride shuts one out. Therefore saving faith comes only through God's revelation.[36]

3. Repentance
   In this passage Christ also gives an all-inclusive invitation as He commands, "Come to me, all who are weary and heavy-laden, and I will give you rest."[37] Though the word repentance is not found specifically, the concept, MacArthur maintains, is clearly there in the phrase "Come to me." It demands a full turn and an absolute change in direction. Therefore saving faith includes repentance.

4. Faith
   MacArthur argues further that the phrase "Come to me" also includes the concept of faith.[38] Repentance is the turning away from sin, and faith is the turning to the Savior.

5. Submission
   The final element of faith from this passage is submission, as stressed in the phrase, "Take my yoke upon you, and learn of me..."[39] The yoke speaks of submission, and the one not willing to surrender to His yoke cannot enter into His saving rest. Salvation clearly comes by grace apart from human works, but the grace of God in salvation brings a faith that includes a submission and willingness to obey.[40] And such submission and obedience is joyous.

Therefore, according to this passage the gospel preached by Jesus and the one we must preach begins with a sovereign God humbling a human heart and revealing His truth to it, whereby that heart turns from sin in repentance and to Christ in faith with a willing and joyous submission.

PRINCIPLE TEN: The gospel preached by Jesus fell on different kinds of hearts and in some cases these hearts appeared to be receptive and to produce true fruit, but in time the fruit proved to be false fruit from an unsaved heart.

The parable of the sower in Matthew 13 is the basis for this principle as expounded by MacArthur.[41] It centered on the preaching of the gospel, as the seed represents the gospel.[42] As the seed is sown (or as the gospel is preached) it falls on different kinds of soil (different kinds of hearts). The wayside soil represents the hardened heart which is totally insensitive to the gospel.[43] The shallow soil represents the superficial response to the gospel, but proves to be false because of no depth of roots, for when the trials

come it fades and withers away.[44]   The weedy soil
represents the worldly heart--the heart consumed by worldly
matters so that the seed of the gospel is choked out.[45] The
good soil represents the heart receptive to the gospel, and it
passes the ultimate test of salvation--the bearing of fruit.[46]

The conclusion of the matter is that only one out of the
four soils is good and it is proved to be good by the fruit it
bears. The weedy soil is a false profession--it never comes
to fruition and never bears fruit. The shallow soil is also a
pretender; and though it looks real at first, it proves to be
false and it never bears fruit. The soil by the wayside is the
clear rejection of the gospel--there is never a profession or
pretense of salvation. The good soil pictures the true
believer, as every believer will ultimately bear fruit--some
more than others, but all will bear some.[47]

Therefore, we can expect the same. Our gospel will fall
onto the same kinds of soil, and some professions will
appear to be genuine converts, and even appear to produce
genuine fruit. But in the passing of time, in some it will
prove to be false fruit from an unsaved heart. Fruitfulness
will be the ultimate test of true salvation.

**PRINCIPLE ELEVEN: The gospel preached by
Jesus produced true fruit, but He was also
aware that Satan could produce counterfeit
converts which from all outward appearance
looked like the real thing.**

The basis for this principle is MacArthur's exposition of
the parable of the wheat and tares in Matthew 13:24-30.[48]
The sower is Christ; the field is the world; the wheat pictures
the true converts; and the tares are Satan's counterfeit.[49]
The fact that the field is the world and not the church has two
thrusts for our thinking.

First, we are to make no effort in the world itself to seek
to rid it by force of the counterfeit tares. That will be the
work of the reapers at Christ's coming.[50]

Second, since the field is the world and not the church, the church does have the responsibility to seek to maintain purity and discipline.[51] To see the church as the field in this parable is a great error and will destroy all the Biblical principles of church discipline.

The issue is the spiritual fruit of each life. Though non-distinguishable to the human eye, that is what distinguishes the two. This is a different matter from anything discussed yet. The tares will also grow in the church and will be outwardly all a Christian would be expected to be in church life and in daily life. We probably couldn't find grounds to accuse or discipline them if we tried.

But again, the principle is the difference in fruit! Looking at both of these parables together, we see false fruit in the lives of all false professors on a scale between the undetectable fruit of the tares to the obvious false fruit of the weedy soil and the shallow soil.

PRINCIPLE TWELVE: The gospel preached by Jesus challenged men to count the cost of entering the kingdom, and yet He also taught that in light of the riches of the kingdom, there is no cost at all.

MacArthur sets forth these principles as he expounds the two parables concerning the treasure of the kingdom in Matthew 13:44-46.[52] In the first parable a man found a treasure in a field, then went and sold all he had so he could purchase that field that he might possess the treasure.[53] The second parable speaks of a man who after a long search found a pearl of great price, for which he was willing to give up everything he owned to obtain it.[54]

What is pictured in these parables is clear. As the sinner comes to see the great treasure and riches to be found in the kingdom of God, he will gladly yield all to receive it. Only God's Spirit can reveal to him the value of the kingdom but when that realization comes in the work of salvation, gladly he gives up all for his Savior.[55] The only reason one would not be willing to make this sacrifice of self and all else would be because he really does not understand the value of God's kingdom.

MacArthur is quick to point out that this does not mean one must literally liquidate all his possessions and take an oath of poverty to be saved.[56] Nor does it indicate that the sinner quits his sins before coming to Christ. Neither does it contradict the fact that salvation is a free gift. But it does mean that salvation impacts a life. In the work of salvation as that life is impacted and transformed the one believing in Christ gives up all for his Savior--a surrender is made which leaves a willingness to do as the Lord demands. Cherished sins are forsaken; precious possessions are turned loose; and secret indulgences are seen as worthless in light of the treasure of the kingdom.

Again, MacArthur points out that the new believer does not fathom all the implications of the fact of Christ's lordship over him, but he has counted the cost and paid the price of death to self.[57]

Thus, as Christ, we must preach the same gospel which challenges men to count the cost to self of entering the kingdom, understanding that as we do preach such a gospel, the Spirit of God will reveal to men that such a price is no cost at all in light of the true riches of the kingdom. As Christ Himself, we must not sanction just any response of the uncommitted,[58] let alone label that response as true salvation.

PRINCIPLE THIRTEEN: The gospel preached by Jesus was a gospel of grace which ruled out any possibility of meriting salvation, and which rescued sinners from the doorstep of hell.

The gospel preached by Jesus, which ruled out any possibility of meriting salvation, meant that there is a possibility of going to hell by one who thinks he stands at the gates of heaven.[59] On the other hand, this same gospel, which is a gospel of grace, can rescue the most deplorable sinner who is sitting on the doorstep of hell. The same grace which shuts out deceived people who think themselves good enough to be saved, ushers into heaven the lost and undeserving sinner who sees his sin and comes to Christ.

These principles are drawn by MacArthur from Christ's parable in Matthew 20:1-16.[60] This is the story of the man who kept hiring laborers at different hours of the day to work in his field, and when the day had ended paid them all the same wage. The point of this parable is that everyone is saved by grace--how long one is saved makes no difference. One saved in his last days on earth is just as completely saved as the one saved early in life, because salvation is by grace and not by merit because of years served.[61]

Further, though MacArthur acknowledges that secondary details of a parable are not primary nor a definite basis for building doctrine, he sees several other truths illustrated in the parable.[62]

1. God, who is sovereign, initiates salvation.

2. God establishes the terms of salvation.

3. God continues to call people to salvation.

4. God's redeemed people work as a result of their salvation.

5. God is compassionate to those who recognize their need.

6. God keeps His promise.

7. God gives by grace more than anyone deserves.

Thus, the parable states, the first shall be last and the last first. The first to enter the kingdom has no more advantage in salvation than the last. The age one enters gives no advantage; the status one holds on earth gives no advantage-- the one who seems to be good must come as a sinner by grace as does the obviously enslaved soul who has been the dupe of Satan and exhibits the debauchery and habits of sin. Grace shuts out the self-righteous, but swings the gate wide to the confessing sinner who comes to Christ.

PRINCIPLE FOURTEEN: The gospel preached by Jesus was a message of repentance, and the worst sinner who repented and turned to Christ would be saved, while the self-righteous man who thought he was good enough to deserve salvation in the eyes of God is excluded from God's favor.

In the three parables of Luke 15 Jesus rebuked the pride of the Pharisees in their self-righteous attitude toward sinners as compared with the sensitive, loving, and compassionate heart of God toward sinners.[63]

The shepherd seeking the lost sheep pictures the Father seeking lost souls.[64] The joy of the shepherd over the rescue of the lost sheep pictures the Father's joy over the rescue of a lost soul. What a contrast with the self-righteous, unconcerned, insensitive Pharisees!

The woman who the lost coin and the joy she had when she found it makes the same point--God is a God who seeks sinners, and what touches Him most deeply is when a sinner is rescued and found.[65] What a contrast again with the cold-hearted, proud Pharisees who looked down on sinners as unworthy of any compassion or concern!

The lost son pictures the same truth, only more graphically in light of the presence in the story of the elder son.[66] What a contrast between the joy of the father and the selfish, self-centered attitude of the elder brother! He would have rather his brother remain in the far country in the ravages of sin than come home to threaten his position and inheritance.

MacArthur sees other truths in this parable as well. The wayward son came home by way of repentance and saving faith.[67] He is a picture of both. He made a complete turn-around; he broke with sin; he made an absolute surrender to his father, which is the essence of saving faith. Clearly he was not the same young man who had left home.

Thus these three parables have common truth which they stress[68]--the seeking God who rejoices to save sinners compared with the attitude of self-righteous Pharisees who have no concern to seek nor to see others saved. God is seeking the lost, and those who come to Him in submissive faith are saved, while those who reject Him in His person and authority because they think they can save themselves by their goodness are lost.

PRINCIPLE FIFTEEN: **The gospel preached by Jesus contained the message of repentance which meant turning from evil to God with an intent to serve Him.**

MacArthur challenges his readers to weigh the gospel preached by Jesus and the contemporary one.[69] Clearly one missing note is repentance. Jesus began His public ministry with a call to repentance (Matthew 4:17). Jesus described His ministry as one of calling sinners to repentance (Luke 5:31). See also His emphasis in Luke 13:3.

However, contemporary preachers dodge the message and necessity of repentance in several ways.[70] Some deny it is part of the gospel message. Others redefine it, saying it is only a change of mind or that it is a synonym for faith. Either way, it cannot mean, according to these men, a change of life.

MacArthur is convinced repentance is far more than the above.[71] The Greek word *metanoia* always speaks of a change of purpose, and specifically a turning from sin.[72] It includes "a repudiation of the old life and a turning to God for salvation."[73] MacArthur sees in I Thessalonians 1:9 three elements in repentance: "a turning to God; a turning from evil; and the intent to serve God."[74] True repentance includes all three of these elements.

Furthermore, MacArthur insists, repentance is not a human work, but rather it is "a sovereignly bestowed gift of repentance

God,"[75] and comes at salvation rather than prior to it. Also
repentance involves the whole man--mind, emotions, and
will.[76] Such repentance also continues throughout the
believer's life (I John 1:9), and is a badge of a true
Christian.[77]

Thus the gospel preached by Jesus included the message
of repentance, that is, a turning to God from sin with the
intent to serve Him.

**PRINCIPLE SIXTEEN: The gospel preached by
    Jesus spoke of a faith which was given by
    God, which also possessed a living and
    abiding quality that gives a will and ability
    to obey.**

The message preached by many, indicates MacArthur, is
a call to come to Jesus as you are, but feel free to stay that
way.[78] According to this view salvation may or may not
alter one's behavior. Thus many respond to such an
invitation, but they are deceived and really do not possess
salvation at all.

MacArthur is convinced that this is the message of James
2:14-26.[79] There does exist such a thing as a dead faith
which has no redemptive character at all. It is a false faith,
mere mental assent, shown to be so by its lack of works,
and is the same as the faith of a demon.

MacArthur points here to the present tense verbs of the
gospel of John in the use of *pisteuo*. This indicates faith is
of a continuing nature and not just an initial act.[80]

Faith, like repentance, is also a gift from God, not the
work of man. As a gift from God it is permanent and
powerful.[81] It will therefore not only transform but it will
abide to the end. Thus God will perfect the work He begins
(Philippians 1:6). The one who possesses true faith will
obey God, though not perfectly.[82]

In fact, faith and obedience are inseparable,[83] as shown
in John 3:36 where they are synonymous (see also Acts 6:7,
Hebrews 5:9, and Hebrews 11:8). This means also that

anyone professing to have faith but who has no obedience does not possess faith at all (Titus 1:15-16).[84] MacArthur spells it out clearly that he is not speaking of any form of sinless perfection.[85]

Thus true faith is a supernatural gift of God with a living and transforming and abiding character, which grants to its possessor a will and desire to obey God. Anything less is not saving faith.

PRINCIPLE SEVENTEEN: **The gospel preached by Jesus offered the choice to a sinner to enter one of two gates: a narrow one found by few, which puts one on the narrow road leading to heaven, or the broad gate which leads to the broad road and eventually to hell. There is no other road nor is there a mingling of the two.**

MacArthur is convinced Matthew 7:13-14 is a devastating blow to modern easy-believism.[86] As the conclusion to the Sermon on the Mount (which he sees as pure gospel and not law), it is clearly the Savior's teaching concerning the way of salvation. In this text we see men making a choice which has definite earthly and eternal results.[87]

The choice each man faces is which gate he will enter-- the narrow gate or the broad gate. If he enters at the narrow gate he journeys on the narrow road which eventually leads to heaven. On the other hand, if he enters at the broad gate he journeys on the broad road which eventually leads to hell. There is no such thing as entering the narrow gate and ending up on the broad road, nor can one enter the broad gate and find himself on the narrow road. The choice a man makes concerning gates determines the road he travels and his final destination. There is no mingling of gates and roads and there is no alternate route.

If anyone thinks salvation is easy, this passage also speaks to that point. Few find the narrow gate and road, while many enter and travel the broad gate and road (see

Luke 13:13, Matthew 11:12, Luke 16:16, I Peter 4:18).[88]
One must remember that it is not human effort which finds
the narrow gate, but by divine grace is one humbled and
broken and led to seek and enter the gate.[89]

Clearly this passage runs counter to the non-lordship
view which has no narrow gate to enter let alone a narrow
road to walk. Neither does it have a pathway to heaven.
Rather, according to the non-lordship view one can be saved
by agreement with the truth of the gospel and then choose
which road to travel. One can expect to find saved on both
roads according to this view.

Thus the Lordship view sees salvation as a choice
between two gates, two roads, two destinations, and that
choice divides mankind clearly into two groups.

**PRINCIPLE EIGHTEEN: The gospel preached by
Jesus included a justification and a sanctification which are distinct but which can never
be separated. Such a separation would allow
sanctification to be optional and would result in believers saying without doing or
hearing without obeying.**

Two key principles concerning the relation of
justification and sanctification must never be forgotten for
the one who seeks theological accuracy, according to
MacArthur.[90] Justification and sanctification must never be
mingled and they must never be separated. To mingle them
is to view our acceptance before God on the basis of our
works. To separate them is to make sanctification optional
rather than a certain result of justification (see Romans 10:10
and Hebrews 12:14). A holiness of life and righteous works
are neither a prerequisite of salvation nor a ground of
salvation, but they are a result of salvation because of the
inseparability of justification and sanctification.

Jesus spoke in Matthew 7:21-23 of those who professed
salvation but refused to do the Father's will.[91] They did
have "religious works," but they failed to do the Father's
will. The doing of the Father's will was not what would

have saved them, but had they been saved they would have done His will. There is a difference.

Jesus was not concerned in this passage if He rattled His hearers' assurance.[92] Self-examination was His goal, and Scripture encourages such in other places (II Corinthians 13:5), especially in light of the fact that many will be in hell who expected to go to heaven. All of this grows from the reality of professing salvation but not doing the will of the Father. Such a one is lost, as it is stated he will be turned away at judgment.

Another possibility is to hear without obeying (Matthew 7:24-27).[93] This is the foolish man who built his house on the sand. He is one of two men who built houses just alike. The only difference was the foundation. Jesus states clearly that the wise man was the man who heard His words, and acted upon them (vs. 24). The other man heard the words, but did not act on them.

Again, this is not saying salvation is by works, but that to truly hear and believe results in the action of obedience. The foolish man's house (the professor) looked good, but when the flood came the false foundation of true spiritual works was unveiled, and great was the collapse of his house.[94]

Thus the gospel preached by Jesus included a justification and sanctification which are distinct, but which are also inseparable, meaning that sanctification is never optional. A true believer's life will not be characterized by a saying but not doing, nor by a hearing without obeying.

PRINCIPLE NINETEEN: The gospel preached by Jesus was a call to discipleship and a true response resulted in confessing Him before men, loving Him before one's own self, and a willingness to die for Him.

The call to salvation and the call to discipleship are part of the same call, according to MacArthur.[95] They are not to be seen as separate, as if the call to discipleship were some later or higher calling. Matthew 28:14-20 sees the work of evangelism as including the making of disciples.[96] The book of Acts uses the terms "disciple" and "believer" as synonyms (see Acts 6:1, 2, 7; 11:26; 14:20, 22; 15:10).[97] Undoubtedly the true Christian is a disciple--discipleship is not optional.[98]

Further, a true disciple has certain characteristics. He will confess Christ before men (Luke 14:32-33).[99] He possesses a love for Christ which is greater than his love for his family or himself (Matthew 10:34-37; Luke 14:26-27). He is willing to lose his life for the sake of Christ (Matthew 10:38-39).[100]

Thus the call to salvation is not a call to a "momentary decision" which is absent of self-denial and commitment. It is a call to a faith which joyfully gives up all for Him.

PRINCIPLE TWENTY: The gospel preached by Jesus presented His whole person, including His lordship. There is no authority in Scripture for one to attempt to accept a divided Lord or to redefine "Lord" to mean deity alone.

MacArthur agrees that the common phrase "making Christ Lord" is not Scriptural.[101] God has already established His Son as Lord (Acts 2:36; Romans 14:9; Philippians 2:11). Men are obligated not to make Him Lord (for they cannot), but they are commanded to bow to His lordship. Anyone who refuses to bow to His lordship is not saved (I Corinthians 12:3; Luke 6:46-49).[102]

Yet many today do not want to include His lordship as part of the gospel message.[103] They maintain that to do so is a violation of a free gospel. They also allow that it is possible to be saved and Christ never become Lord.

To refute this contention MacArthur argues that Jesus often made His lordship the key issue with lost sinners.[104] This is evidenced in the rich young ruler in Matthew 19, and also in Matthew 7:21-22 and Luke 6:46-49. Jesus as Lord is a central part of the gospel message.

Furthermore, the term "Jesus is Lord" means several things. It declares first of all "that He is almighty God, the Creator and sustainer of all things" (Colossians 1:17).[105] It also means that Christ is sovereign (Matthew 12:8; John 5:17-18, 5:19-47, 10:22-42, 10:17-18, 5:22; Philippians 2:11-12, etc.).[106] It speaks of "dominion, authority, sovereignty, and the right to govern."[107] Any attempt to redefine "Lord" to mean anything less is incorrect.[108]

Clearly to call men to Christ is to call them to all He is, and therefore it is to call men to His lordship.[109] One cannot separate the saviorhood of Christ from His total person and call men to that partial aspect of His person.

The Biblical invitations in Acts never severed one aspect of His person from another. In fact, the New Testament invitations include His lordship (Acts 2:21, 2:36, 16:31; Romans 10:9-10).[110]

Therefore, argues MacArthur, the "signature of saving faith is surrender to the lordship of Christ."[111] Also the real evidence that one belongs to Christ is a willingness to submit to Christ's authority. This is not to argue for a gospel of works, for only God can enable a man to acknowledge His lordship.[112] Clearly the non-lordship view is not consistent here. The salvation they offer does not necessarily offer deliverance from the power of sin because they have no Lord of authority and dominion to offer to sinners--only a Jesus who is Savior.

PRINCIPLE TWENTY-ONE: **The gospel preached by Jesus is the same gospel which was preached by the apostles, and therefore it is a grave error to set the two against one another in any way or for any purpose.**

MacArthur strongly opposes any attempt to argue for non-lordship salvation on a basis which would set Christ against the apostles simply because Jesus' message was prior to the cross.[113]

All of the apostles in one way or another support and agree with the message of Jesus concerning the lordship of Christ in salvation, the place of works in the Christian's life, the presence of perseverance as an evidence of true salvation, the place of repentance in the gospel transaction, etc.[114]

Rather than a disunity in the New Testament between authors on the content of the gospel message, there is a marvelous unity that we also must recognize and uphold in our ministry of the gospel.

PRINCIPLE TWENTY-TWO: The gospel preached by Jesus is the same gospel preached by historic Christianity.

Making use of writers and theologians of church history, as well as the confessions of faith and other key doctrinal documents, MacArthur argues that the Lordship gospel is the same gospel preached by historic Christianity.[115] This means that non-lordship salvation is a modern heresy which is outside the mainstream of the historic Christian faith.

SUMMARY AND CONCLUSION

Again, in order to see all the principles of the MacArthur Lordship view as stated above, they are listed below.

1. The gospel preached by Jesus is a far-cry from the gospel preached by many today.

2. The gospel preached by Jesus called for nothing short of the transformation brought by regeneration or the new birth.

3   The gospel preached by Jesus resulted in men and women worshipping Him, and therefore a true response to the gospel includes a submissive, worshipful heart.

4. The gospel preached by Jesus was a gospel that deals with sin--He came to forgive and deliver the sinner from his sins.

5. The gospel which Jesus preached called for more than an intellectual assent to certain facts, but it involved a divine miracle which opened blind spiritual eyes and gave a new heart.

6. The gospel preached by Jesus included the proclamation of the law so men would understand their sin and the necessity of turning from it as they turned to Christ in faith.

7. The gospel preached by Jesus radically changed men and their actions following an encounter with Him, and such an experience left no doubt about the reality of their salvation.

8. The gospel preached by Jesus at times encountered hardened hearts which professed faith in Him, but which proved later by their lives that they were not true believers.

9. The gospel preached by Jesus rested on the sovereign will of God and the faithful preaching of a saving faith which included humility, revelation, repentance, faith, and submission.

10. The gospel preached by Jesus fell on different kinds of hearts and in some cases these hearts appeared to be receptive and to produce true fruit, but in time the fruit proved to be false fruit from an unsaved heart.

11. The gospel preached by Jesus produced true fruit, but He was also aware that Satan could produce counterfeit converts which from all outward appearance looked like the real thing.

12. The gospel preached by Jesus challenged men to count the cost of entering the kingdom, and yet He also taught that in light of the riches of the kingdom, there is no cost at all.

13. The gospel preached by Jesus was a gospel of grace which ruled out any possibility of meriting salvation, and which rescued sinners from the doorstep of hell.

14. The gospel preached by Jesus was a message of repentance, and the worst sinner who repented and turned to Christ would be saved, while the self-righteous man who thought he was good enough to deserve salvation in the eyes of God is excluded from God's favor.

15. The gospel preached by Jesus contained the message of repentance which meant turning from evil to God with an intent to serve Him.

16. The gospel preached by Jesus spoke of a faith which was given by God, which also possessed a living and abiding quality that gives a will and ability to obey.

17. The gospel preached by Jesus offered the choice to a sinner to enter one of two gates: a narrow one found by few, which puts one on the narrow road leading to heaven, or the broad gate which leads to the broad road and eventually to hell. There is no other road nor is there a mingling of the two.

18. The gospel preached by Jesus included a justification and a sanctification which are distinct but which can never be separated. Such a separation would allow sanctification to be optional and would result in believers saying without doing or hearing without obeying.

19. The gospel preached by Jesus was a call to discipleship, and a true response resulted in confessing Him before

men, loving Him before one's own self, and a willingness to die for Him.

20. The gospel preached by Jesus presented His whole person, including His lordship. There is no authority in Scripture for one to attempt to accept a divided Lord or to redefine "Lord" to mean deity alone.

21. The gospel preached by Jesus is the same gospel which was preached by the apostles, and therefore it is a grave error to set the two against one another in any way or for any purpose.

22. The gospel preached by Jesus is the same gospel preached by historic Christianity.

PART TWO

A Comparison of the Two Sides

of the Controversy

CHAPTER 3

A THEOLOGICAL COMPARISON OF LORDSHIP AND NON-LORDSHIP SALVATION

By now the reader should have concluded that there is a great difference in Lordship and non-lordship salvation. In fact the difference is almost antithetical in many instances. To help the reader see the contrasts, the next two chapters will be comparative. First the main theological subject areas will be contrasted, and then the important Scripture passages and the comparative exegetical handling of them will be examined. Brevity will be attempted, but not guaranteed at every subject area.

I. SALVATION

A. Lordship Salvation

Salvation is by grace through faith, and such salvation includes repentance from sin and a turning to Christ in faith, submitting to His person and His authority over one's life. These are accompaniments and results of salvation and not conditions of salvation. Thus one who is saved will give evidence of it.

B. Non-Lordship Salvation

Salvation is by grace through faith alone and nothing else. Such faith does not include repentance from sin or any submission to His person or authority over one's life. Any other viewpoint which insists salvation includes repentance or submission to Christ is adding the conditions of human works to salvation and therefore is a salvation by contract or works. Thus the one who is saved may or may not give evidence of it.

II.   FAITH

A.   Lordship Salvation

Faith is the response of the whole person to the Lord Jesus Christ. It includes a mental aspect as one hears and understands the facts of the gospel. It includes an emotional aspect as one realizes the eternal consequences of the gospel in relation to one's life and sin. It also includes a volitional aspect as one agrees with and responds to the truth, content, and person of the message of the gospel.

B.   Non-Lordship Salvation

Faith is to believe the facts of the gospel. That is, it is to take God at His word concerning the truth content of the gospel. Add anything else to faith as an accompaniment or as a result, and it is no longer saving faith. Thus faith can exist without repentance, without submission, without works, without perseverance, without discipleship, etc. Faith even exists if it does not continue, for it is a one-time act which affects eternal life forever. Faith should continue, but it doesn't always; but in either case its effect is irreversible.

III.   REPENTANCE

A.   Lordship Salvation

Repentance is an integral part of saving faith. It includes a change of mind, but it is more than that. It is a turning from sin and a turning to Christ by faith with the purpose of serving Him. It is a gift of God and not a work of man. Though it is a part of saving faith, it is also the continuous attitude and action of a Christian. It is a part of the gospel message, and any claim to preach the gospel which omits repentance is a false claim.

B. Non-Lordship Salvation

Repentance is not an integral part of saving faith. In fact, it is no part of saving faith. It is not restricted to the lost or even to the moment of salvation. The call to repentance has to do with a harmonious relation to God and not to salvation. Repentance, or this harmonious relation to God, can precede salvation or it can follow salvation. It can precede salvation by several years or it can follow salvation by several years. There is the possibility that one can be saved and never experience repentance. One can even be a repentant unbeliever or an unrepentant believer. Repentance has to do with harmony and fellowship with God and not with salvation.

IV. REGENERATION

A. Lordship Salvation

Regeneration is the supernatural work of God whereby the sinner is transformed by the giving of new life in Christ. As a result of this new life there will also be certain changes in the saved sinner's life. There will be deliverance from the dominion of sin and a desire and power to live a godly life. It would be impossible for one to experience regeneration and remain unchanged. Transformation is the heart and evidence of regeneration.

B. Non-Lordship Salvation

Regeneration is the supernatural work of God whereby the sinner is imparted new life, but there is not necessarily the transformation of life. Changes may take place or they may not take place in the life of the new convert. There may be the power of deliverance over the authority and dominion of sin or there may not be. There may be a power to live a godly life and there may not be. It could be possible to experience regeneration and remain unchanged. Transformation is not necessarily the heart or evidence of salvation.

V.   ASSURANCE

A.   Lordship Salvation

Assurance of salvation is of great blessing and encouragement to the believer, and Scripture gives glorious promise of God's power to save and keep. Yet the believer should not take his salvation for granted nor presume upon the grace of God. Scripture challenges us to examine ourselves to see that we are in the faith. The evidence we are His is the presence of a holy and godly life and godly works. The absence of such should cause deep and serious examination of life to see if we really have experienced saving faith. Such examination should result in a renewed commitment to godliness or in a true experience of salvation and saving faith.

B.   Non-Lordship Salvation

Assurance of salvation is of great blessing and benefit to the believer, but it can never be based on the presence or absence of good works. As one is born again and as new life is imparted by the Word, and as saving faith is experienced, assurance of salvation comes to the individual as well. Saving faith and assurance are inseparable. To believe God's Word about Christ is simultaneous with the experience of assurance. The acceptance of the content of the gospel message brings with it the certainty and guarantee of assurance. To doubt the message is to doubt the possession of eternal life. To doubt the possession of eternal life is to doubt the message. The one-time aspect of faith should be remembered at this point as was discussed under the heading 'Faith'. It is not that one continues to have assurance as one continues to believe or to walk in faith. It is that one has assurance based on the initial, one-time experience of saving faith.

VI. PERSEVERANCE

A. Lordship Salvation

Perseverance speaks of the continuance of the true believer in faith and godliness. This is not to say that the true believer will never grow cold or backslide. It is to say that the life-style of the believer will in the passing of time evidence godliness and holiness. It is also to say that what God has begun in the believer by the power of His Holy Spirit, He will continue and perfect. Thus the true believer will continue and persevere. To fail to persevere over a period of time without chastisement and discipline proves one is not a true possessor of salvation.

B. Non-Lordship Salvation

Perseverance is the badge and evidence of success in the Christian life, not the badge and evidence of the presence or absence of true saving faith. To say that salvation guarantees perseverance is incorrect, for the Christian can fail to live for Christ and he could even apostatize. Yet this failure or a series of failures or a life of failure or even a life of apostasy has nothing to do with the possession or lack of possession of eternal life. It only has to do with success or failure in living the Christian life. The Christian life is a battle and the Christian can lose the battle (even every day of his life), but he cannot lose his possession of eternal life.

VII.   DISCIPLESHIP

A.   Lordship Salvation

The call to salvation is also a call to discipleship. The two cannot and must not be separated. To distinguish between the two is unbiblical in that it creates a false dichotomy in the evangelistic message and method of the Lord Jesus. Such a false division which makes two calls out of the one Biblical call will create great confusion in the church since it will promote a concept of salvation without commitment and discipleship. It will comfort lost people to think they are saved while they languish in sin and unbelief. Faith must never be separated from discipleship. The call Christ gave to sinners included both.

B.   Non-Lordship Salvation

Salvation and discipleship are two distinct matters in the Bible and the call to one must never be confused or mingled with the call to the other. Discipleship is hard and difficult while salvation is free. Thus we must call men to salvation first, and then after they have received the gospel message we speak to them of discipleship. To mix the two might cause them to trust their commitment to discipleship as part of their salvation, which would be a salvation by works and therefore no salvation at all.

Discipleship is a process of education and therefore could not be part of the salvation call. Believers must grow in discipleship, while salvation is instantaneous. There is no evidence in the Bible that the educational process of discipleship will be automatically produced in all believers. It is possible that one can be a believer all his life and never enroll in the school of discipleship. The believer is encouraged to think very seriously about the cost of discipleship and only enter that course after understanding the reality of its difficulty. In a real sense, discipleship is optional.

VIII. OBEDIENCE AND WORKS

A.   Lordship Salvation

Though obedience and works are not the basis nor the cause of salvation, they are clearly related to salvation. True salvation will result in a life of obedience and godly works. It is incredible to think one can experience the power of regeneration and all the other accompaniments of salvation by grace and still possess a rebel's heart and a rebel's lifestyle. Certainly the new believer has much to learn and much growth to experience, but the rebel's heart has been replaced by a submissive believing heart, and a similar lifestyle will follow. Obedience and works, therefore, are not optional in the Christian life, they are the evidence of true salvation.   Anyone who professes salvation while possessing an unbeliever's or rebel's lifestyle may very well be presuming the grace of God which he does not really possess.

B.   Non-Lordship Salvation

Obedience and works are not the basis nor the cause of salvation, nor are they related to the evidence or proof of one's salvation. True salvation will not necessarily result in a life of obedience and godly works. To make them an evidence or proof of salvation is to preach a salvation of works-righteousness and not faith alone. Therefore, it is possible for one to be saved and yet have no fruit or works to follow. Growth and fruit are hoped for but still optional for the believer. It is possible not only to profess salvation but also to possess salvation while continually evidencing a rebel's heart and an unbeliever's lifestyle.

IX.   APOSTASY

A.   Lordship Salvation

Apostasy is the total rejection of the Christian faith and a return to a non-Christian lifestyle. Because of the nature of saving faith, the power of regeneration, and the doctrine of perseverance, the true believer cannot totally and finally apostatize. God has pledged Himself to His people in Christ and they will persevere. If one apostatizes, that is proof such a one was never truly saved. God does not grant security to those who merely profess to know Christ, but to those who truly know Him. No matter how spectacular or full of fireworks one's profession and early work is, when such a one becomes an apostate, he proves he never was a Christian.

B.   Non-Lordship Salvation

Apostasy is possible for a true Christian. Since salvation is by a faith, which is defined as an agreement with God concerning the truth content of the gospel, and since in salvation there is not necessarily any turning from sin or commitment in discipleship, it is therefore conceivable that a true Christian can apostatize. Clearly it is possible for a Christian to fail and it is also possible for him to fail completely.

Other areas of doctrine could be compared, but these key ones we have considered should be sufficient to show both sides of the controversy and also convince the reader of the antithetical nature of the two theologies. We now turn to compare each side's exposition of several key passages of Scripture.

CHAPTER 4

A SCRIPTURAL COMPARISON OF LORDSHIP AND NON-LORDSHIP SALVATION

Not only is it helpful to contrast Lordship and non-lordship salvation in their primary theological beliefs, but it is also helpful to understand how they handle various Scriptural passages in comparison. Again the antithetical nature of the controversy will be evident as this comparison unfolds.

I.   LUKE 15:11-32---THE PRODIGAL SON

A.   Lordship Salvation

The prodigal son evidences repentance in the work of salvation in an individual's life. He sensed his need. He admitted he had done wrong. He possessed a heart and spirit of repentance. He turned from sin to the father. He submitted himself to the father and whatever he commanded or willed. He is a solid example of true saving faith.

B.   Non-Lordship Salvation

The prodigal son is an evidence of salvation by faith alone, which faith does not include repentance or submission to the authority of Christ. He came to his senses, but all he said at this point in the far country is typical of the sinner who thinks we must work to be saved. He did not understand that acceptance with the father was unconditional--absolutely free. The prodigal returned home, but never got to make his works-oriented speech, for the father accepted him completely by grace. The bargain he had planned to make with his father never came to pass for its need was negated by the power of grace. To think the father would have predicated reception of the son on his willingness to work is inconceivable. Clearly Luke 15 negates Lordship salvation and establishes the non-lordship view.

II. JAMES 2:14-26--FAITH WITHOUT WORKS IS DEAD!

A. Lordship Salvation

When James states that "faith without works is dead," he is stating that any profession of faith which does not evidence itself by the presence of Christian works is a false faith. Such a false faith is not a true saving faith. Such a faith is akin to the faith of the demons, which is a mental assent. Undeniably faith for James includes more than believing the facts or truth content of the gospel.

B. Non-Lordship Salvation

When James states that "faith without works is dead," he is not stating that there are two kinds of faith--a true saving faith and a false, non-saving faith. Rather he is saying that there are two kinds of faith among Christians--an active one (the true faith which has works) and the dead one (the true faith which is producing no works). After all, James is writing to believers; and he is not challenging them to judge their salvation by the presence or absence of works, but to stir them to an active faith as Christians. It is an active saving faith which is evidenced by works as compared to an inactive saving faith which is evidenced by a lack of works. The presence or absence of salvation is not an issue here.

What about the use of the word "dead" in James 2? Does that not evidence one is speaking of a spurious non-saving faith? No, that which is said to be dead was at one time alive. Therefore, the term "dead" cannot be speaking of a non-saving faith for such a faith was never alive. It must be speaking of an inactive or "dead" faith of a believer, for such a faith was alive at one point.

What about the question in James 2:14, "Can faith save him?" That is, can this kind of faith which possesses no works be a saving faith? The word "save" here does not speak of salvation from hell. Rather it refers to deliverance from physical death, especially in light of the fact that James is addressing believers. An inactive, or dead, faith can lead to physical death.

The conclusion, therefore, is that works are not an evidence of salvation, neither is the absence of works an evidence of one not possessing salvation. James 2 has nothing to do with salvation at all.

III. ROMANS 10:9-13--"WHOSOEVER SHALL CALL ON THE NAME OF THE LORD SHALL BE SAVED"

A. Lordship Salvation

Many Scriptures could be marshalled to show that the lordship of Christ is an integral part of the gospel message, but few are as clear as Romans 10:9-13. If one confesses with his mouth Jesus as Lord, and believes in his heart that God raised Him from the dead--that one shall be saved (vs. 9). Could it be any clearer? Recognition of Jesus as Lord is part of the gospel. Also, verse 13 declares that whoever calls on the name of the Lord shall be saved. To seek to rob the gospel message of His lordship is clearly contrary to Scripture.

B. Non-Lordship Salvation

Calling on the name of the Lord in Scripture is not something unbelievers do, but it is a privilege of Christians. Early believers called on the name of the Lord for every situation and problem of life. It was this calling on the name of the Lord by believers which Paul was referring to in Romans 10. This is not a salvation passage. It speaks of a Christian activity. A careful consideration of verses 14-15 makes that clear. The order here is undeniable. The preacher is sent. Following his sending, he preaches. Following his preaching, people hear. Following their hearing, people believe. Following belief, people call on the name of the Lord. Undeniably in this sequence faith must precede calling on Him. That is, faith must obviously precede a believer calling on Him for help and deliverance in life.

IV.   JOHN 4--THE WOMAN AT THE WELL

A.   Lordship Salvation

The woman at the well also gives guidance in understanding the nature of saving faith and its results, even though little is stated about her thoughts and emotions throughout her confrontation with Christ. The text doesn't even state clearly that she was saved, but we can draw some inferences from her words and actions. When she hurried to tell others of her encounter with Christ, it can be assumed that she had been touched by her experience with Him. Had she not faced the reality of her sin as Christ reminded her of an immoral life? Had Christ not revealed Himself to her? Did she not go and herald His person to others? Is not the change in her life evident to the men of the city with whom she shares her witness? Did not the men she witnessed to, when they had believed, refer to Christ as the Savior of the world?

Thus in the encounter between Christ and the woman sin is a reality to her, a change of life is evident, a joy so great over her experience is present that she must tell others, and Christ is seen as Savior (Savior from what, if not from sin?). Scripture does not tell us everything, but it tells us enough to see the expected elements of saving faith.

B.   Non-Lordship Salvation

The woman at the well sets before us the simplicity and the one-timeness of saving faith. She was told she needed to drink only once from the water of life and her thirst would be satisfied forever. Jesus did not tell her she had to drink on and on but rather a single initial drink would bring water springing up in her soul forever. She did not need to drink continually (believe continually) the water (salvation) to prove her salvation was real. The simplicity of the one drink brought eternal life forever.

Obvious here also is the absence of any attempt by Christ to pull from her any promise to quit her sin or straighten up her immoral life before she could be saved. The water is hers freely if she wants it. Any hidden or stated conditions would have ruined the gospel offer. Also absent is any attempt by Christ to challenge her to recognize or submit to His lordship.   The absence of such conditions is understandable in light of the fact that He is offering her a free gift. Finally the woman possesses an assurance not based on her future works (we don't even know if she broke with her immoral life), but on the basis of the promise of the gospel.

V.   I JOHN--TESTS OF WHAT?

A.   Lordship Salvation

The book of I John contains a series of tests whereby the church and its people can know who is truly saved and who is not. Within the pages of this epistle one will find doctrinal tests which center on the person of Christ, and also ethical tests which center on our life and walk. Both are necessary and helpful for determining salvation.

B.   Non-Lordship Salvation

The book of I John does contain tests, but they are tests
of fellowship and not tests of salvation. Since the readers
were saved and had the promise of eternal life, nothing could
threaten them nor rob them of salvation. But their
fellowship with the Lord would be endangered by moral and
doctrinal threats. Therefore the danger John warns against is
the seduction of the believer by immorality and doctrinal
error which would rob him of his fellowship with God.

VI.   JOHN 9--THE MAN BORN BLIND

A.   Lordship Salvation

The man healed by Jesus who had been born blind is an
example of the power of God to save sinners from the power
of sin. As God is able to bring physical eyesight, so
salvation is by the power of God as He brings spiritual life
and sight. But the blind man is also an example of a
submissive heart in salvation. In the evolution of his
understanding of Christ he moved from seeing Him as a man
to recognizing Him as "Lord" (vs. 37-38). God had opened
his blind eyes and in response he bowed and worshipped
Christ. Surely this was a recognition and submission to the
person and authority of Christ, for the very heart and core of
worship is submission.

B.   Non-Lordship Salvation

The man born blind who was healed by Christ is an
example of salvation by faith alone--a faith whose nature is
only a recognition of the truth of the gospel. There is no
repentance in this story nor is there any mention of
submission to Christ. The only need of the man as he stood
before Christ was information so he could then have saving
faith. This Christ gave him and he was saved.

VII. MATTHEW 19:16-22--THE RICH YOUNG RULER

A. Lordship Salvation

The rich young ruler's key problem as he came to Christ seeking life was that he had no sense of sin. Anyone who thinks he has kept the law of God perfectly not only misunderstands the law, but also misunderstands himself as a sinner before a holy God. Christ's command to sell all and follow Him was indicative that the sinner must meet Christ's terms--he must not expect Christ to meet his terms. But Christ's command also was a challenge to his claim to have kept the law perfectly, so that through the command he could see Christ's person and authority. Who else but God has the right to make such a command? And if God is making this command on him, and if he is a perfect keeper of the law will he not obey it? It was not that the keeping of the command would save him, but that his failure would show him his sin in the presence of a divine command. The young man refused to see the truth and therefore never knew salvation by grace.

B. Non-Lordship Salvation

Even though Jesus' encounter with the rich young ruler included an invitation to discipleship along with a call to massive self-sacrifice, we must not confuse this with the central plank of Christ's evangelistic message and thrust. Christ does challenge him to sacrifice everything to be His disciple and he would receive a rich reward in heaven. But this was for the most part to unveil his self-righteous pride, and to cause him to contemplate the person of Christ and conclude His deity. Clearly it was necessary for him to place his faith in Christ first, before he could seriously consider this extreme call to discipleship. Therefore, though Christ called him to discipleship, it was only a secondary call which must follow the response by faith to the person of

Christ, but it could also help him to see the need of faith response alone as the way of salvation.

Again, numerous other verses in the controversy could be discussed, but as in the subject comparison, we have sought to deal with the major ones.   Others will be mentioned in the next and final chapters of critique.

PART THREE

A Critique of

Non-Lordship Salvation

CHAPTER 5

STRAW MEN

If one were to suggest that the time would come when a group of evangelical Christians would be arguing for a salvation without repentance, without a change of behavior or lifestyle, without a real avowal of the lordship and authority of Christ, without perseverance, without discipleship, and a salvation which does not necessarily result in obedience and works, and with a regeneration which does not necessarily change one's life, most believers of several decades ago would have felt such would be an absolute impossibility. But believe it or not, the hour has come.

How has such a concept of salvation come to pass? How could multitudes become convinced of such a view of salvation? It has been conceived by a group of sincere men who have argued this position in a very convincing manner. Not only are these men sincere, but they are scholars who are able to discuss the intricacies of the original language and other exegetical factors in a persuasive manner.

Yet as this author has studied the logic, the exegesis, the arguments and statements of Hodges in his book, it has been concluded that the non-lordship position he presents is based on straw men, exegetical inaccuracies, flawed theological thinking, and some illogical and unbelievable statements. Perhaps some readers at this point will stop reading the book. If one does, it may very well mean that such a reader is fearful of a careful examination of his position lest it is shown to be standing on a defenseless foundation. If the truth is at stake, and it is, one should be willing to consider arguments against his position. The outcome will be beneficial either way as the reader is either further established in his original position, convinced of its truthfulness; or he will change his position, having been persuaded his original view was erroneous.

The discussion begins with a few of the numerous straw men which are evident in Hodges' discussion and presentation of the Lordship position. A straw man is the incorrect and erroneous presentation of your opponent's view so that you can argue against it and destroy its validity more easily. The only problem is that the destruction of a straw man is not the destruction of your opponent's view. It is only the destruction of a straw man. Hodges' argumentation against Lordship salvation is filled with straw man conclusions. These are not just differences of interpretations of various passages, but they are false accusations against another's position to gain an unfair advantage in debate. Extended discussion could be devoted to each of these straw men but for the sake of space an attempt at brevity will be made as we deal with a few.

1. Lordship salvation is a system of works-righteousness.

Hodges is convinced that Lordship salvation is a way of salvation that is akin to the works-righteousness system of Roman Catholic dogma.[1] It is a form of legal salvation which says "This do and thou shalt live."[2] The reason he draws this conclusion is his premise that all results and accompaniments of saving faith must be looked upon as means of salvation. Because he sees these as means, he then concludes Lordship salvation is advocating a contract of works between God and man as the way of salvation.

Cannot the reader see this as a straw man? Lordship salvation sees true saving faith as by grace alone. Faith is the means of salvation--faith alone. But such saving faith has certain characteristics and certain accompaniments. The character of saving faith is more than an inward conviction of the truth content of the gospel. Such an inward conviction involves and includes, or will result in, actions which reflect such a convincement. If not, that inward conviction is no more than a mental assent. Though Hodges does not like this term of mental or intellectual assent,[3] he never clearly distinguishes his view from it. Surely the reader can see that if it is a choice between mental assent and a saving faith which includes the involvement of the whole man and not just his mind, the latter is the Biblical view of faith.

Furthermore, Lordship salvation does not make works or obedience the means of salvation but a result, and that is a far-cry difference from the accusation and straw man erected by Hodges. Surely the reader can see the difference between "results" and "means." Anyone who refuses to make this distinction but rather makes the results the basis of a contract with God, is clearly erecting a straw man.

In summary, the controversy between Lordship and non-lordship salvation centers on the nature and results of saving faith. The non-lordship view states that saving faith is no more than an inward conviction of the truth content of the gospel and it brings no certain results. Lordship salvation says that the character of saving faith involves the whole man. Since the whole man is involved, man's will as well as his mind responds positively to the gospel. Such a response of the whole man brings the results of Christian obedience and works. This is not a works-righteousness view of salvation. It is the Biblical view of salvation by faith alone, and it gives faith its full definition and results.

2. Lordship salvation has lost confidence in the power of God.

This accusation comes out in a discussion by Hodges centering on Lordship salvation's concern over the results of his view of the nature of saving faith.[4] Lordship salvation fears, he indicates, that to preach his view of faith will produce converts without changed lives and therefore bring an impurity to the church. The remedy at this point, according to Hodges, is to rely on the power of God to prevent this. But he indicates in other places that we cannot be sure the power of God will remedy the problem. The power of God guarantees nothing--it is completely the choice of the believer whether after salvation he yields to Christ, follows Christ, serves Christ, or lives a life pleasing to

Christ.[5] If the power of God really guarantees certain
results, then Hodges himself is holding here (according to
his definition, not this author's) to a works-righteousness
salvation.

Furthermore, Lordship salvation has not lost its faith in
the power of God. Lordship salvation believes in the power
of God in salvation to change the sinner's life as he comes to
Christ. Lordship salvation sees the power of God to change
both life and behavior; to produce holiness and godliness; to
bring works and obedience. Non-lordship salvation does
not.

Thus it is non-lordship salvation which has lost
confidence in the power of God to change lives--not
Lordship salvation. For Hodges to claim to trust the power
of God to produce results is a major inconsistency, which
contradicts his basic and fundamental plank of his entire
system. He is stating that we can trust the power of God to
produce obedience and works and keep the church from
corruption. This is what Lordship salvation says--a view
Hodges himself labels as works-righteousness, for all
results must be seen as a means of salvation.

3. Lordship salvation has no room for failure and therefore lays a foundation for defeat.

Hodges is convinced that the Christian is locked in a real
battle, and he can fail. He can even apostatize.[6] But
Lordship salvation, which insists that obedience and
perseverance are the proofs of salvation, does not allow for
failure. In not allowing for failure, it lays a certain
foundation for defeat, for as one fails he will conclude he is
lost and therefore give up the fight.

In this discussion Hodges fails to present the Lordship
view accurately, therefore he is erecting a straw man. The
Lordship position does allow for failure. Christians do sin.
They can sin grievously. They can backslide. They can be
cold and inactive for a time. These are failures--serious
failures.

Further, this writer knows of no Lordship salvation adherent who challenges one to question his or her salvation at one point of failure or defeat. Hodges seems to indicate falsely that each time a Christian fails, he himself or some advocate of Lordship thinking will be there telling him he has never been saved or that he must question at this point the reality of his salvation. Such is not the case.

True, Lordship salvation does not believe in a Christian apostatizing from the faith. Yet, on the other hand, the position does not deny the reality and possibility of failure. But such failure will not be a constant and continual pattern of life over an extended period of time without the power of God's perseverance restoring such a one or the hand of God's discipline chastening that individual. If there is no chastening or discipline, that one is not saved. It is at this point of extended failure and defeat that such a professing Christian must be faced with the possibility he is not truly saved but only presuming the grace of God. Prior to this, it is always well and proper for the believer to make his calling and election sure (II Peter 1:10).

Thus, counter to Hodges' straw man, the Lordship view does leave room for failure, but not apostasy. Neither does it lay a foundation for defeat.

4. Lordship salvation spoils troop morale and leads to defeat.

Obviously this straw man is built on the previous straw man, which makes it a dual straw man. Hodges contends that if an army is discouraged, it will also be demoralized and will find fighting difficult, with defeat a probability.[7] Since Lordship salvation encourages one to question his salvation and to judge the reality of his profession by victorious living, will not the Christian soldier be discouraged when he does not live victoriously? How and why therefore can he fight the battle? Thus Lordship salvation discourages the troops and causes them to lose the desire for battle. Non-lordship salvation assures the individual he is saved regardless of how he lives or how he might fail and thus he will fight and keep fighting in the face of the most serious defeats.

Again, Hodges' reasoning is fallacious. His view does not build morale as he claims but destroys it. He has an army with no commitment, no submission to its Captain, and fighting and self-sacrifice are optional. What guarantee does he have that out of all that defeat there will be any desire to keep on fighting? What will that do to troop morale?

Are not many pastors (the officers of the army) discouraged by the lack of commitment by the troops and by the continual pouring of the uncommitted into the army? Are not many of the troops discouraged by the lack of reality of numerous professors which never carry through to give evidence of salvation? Are not many of the spiritual army disappointed and discouraged when they see members of their rank consorting with the enemy, doing the works of the enemy but still claiming they are part of the spiritual army and encouraged to think so by some leaders of the troops? Are not many of the professing Christians who live ungodly lives entrenched in those lives by the comforting thought that they are truly saved, regardless of how they might live?

Lordship salvation doesn't spoil the troop morale--it will build it by setting and upholding the standards and discipline of the spiritual army. Non-lordship salvation spoils the troop morale by allowing an army without character, commitment, submission to authority, and individual discipline.

5. Lordship salvation takes away the shield of faith from the Christian warrior.

Hodges further accuses Lordship salvation of taking away the believer's shield of faith.[8] Ephesians 6:16 tells us the believer must defend himself from the fiery darts of Satan by his faith--his shield of faith. But what if the believer comes to doubt his faith, as Lordship salvation encourages. Will that not weaken his shield or even take it completely from him? Should he not, instead of questioning his shield, be confident of it so he can wield it in battle against Satan's flaming darts?

Again, this is easily seen to be a straw man. Sometimes Hodges speaks as if all Lordship salvation does is cause doubt of salvation. Proponents of Lordship salvation would agree with the importance of faith in the battle, but they would also see the ineffectual and even destructive character of a false faith. How can a false faith stand in battle against Satan? Will it not go on suffering defeat, while all the time being told by Hodges never to question its reality but to press on in battle while it goes from one defeat to another? How could such a one come out of this defeat except by facing the question of the truth or falsity of his salvation?

Or what about the true believer and his faith? Wouldn't he be better prepared to ward off Satan's threatening darts with a strong faith (a strong shield) than with a weak or cracked shield or even one full of holes? Does not Lordship salvation challenge him to test his shield and repair it for battle, if necessary?

Lordship salvation does not take the believer's shield from him, but strengthens his shield, while non-lordship salvation sends him into battle with an untested shield--or for the unsaved professor, with no shield at all, but with the deception he has one.

Again the reader is left to decide who grants the stronger and more dependable shield for battle.

6. Lordship salvation baptizes the American success ethic into the church.

As one reads the Hodges book, one wonders what logic could bring statements of this kind--that Lordship salvation "baptizes the American success ethic into the church."[9] He says further in this context that Lordship salvation tells us that "God . . . is the God only of the spiritually successful." What is one to make of this statement?

If this writer understands the American success ethics, it consists of a mentality that elevates success to the forefront with an immunity towards any concern as to how one arrives at that point of success. Yes, success is the ultimate goal, but part and parcel of that ethic is an unconcern for the means or pathway travelled to arrive at the goal.

It may be true that Lordship salvation wants professing converts to live victorious and godly lives, but no doubt so does non-lordship salvation. But it is not true that Lordship salvation is unconcerned about the pathway to that success. Lordship salvation advocates that the pathway to that success is discipline, commitment, godliness, and spirituality, not as part of salvation, but as a necessity to reach the ultimate goal. They are confident they serve a God of power who will bring His people to the ultimate goal. This is hardly the American success ethic which exalts man and his power and his ruthless abandon to reach a selfish goal.

CONCLUSION

The above are a few of the straw men Hodges presents in an effort to strengthen his case. Any theological debater would do well to abstain from such caustic accusations and obvious straw men, for these only weaken his own case and raise a question as to his confidence in his own position.

We now turn to speak of the exegetical inaccuracies and inconsistencies of the non-lordship system.

CHAPTER 6

EXEGETICAL INACCURACIES AND INCONSISTENCIES

Besides the straw men which Hodges raises to strengthen his case for non-lordship salvation, his position also contains numerous exegetical problems. Having established a false view of saving faith, he must twist passages to fit his system. In this setting it is impossible to list them all, but a sufficient number will be cited and refuted to give the reader an idea of the exegetical inaccuracies that abound in his book.

1. The English equivalency of Greek words.

In his discussion of saving faith, Hodges argues that the English words "believe" and "faith" which render their Greek counterparts are "fully adequate equivalents."[1] To deny this is to "betray an inadequate or misguided view of biblical linguistics."[2] "To believe" must be allowed to mean "to believe."

This contention raises several questions. First, are we certain of the exact meaning of "believe" in the English? Does the word "believe" in English always bear to us the same meaning? For Hodges, to have faith is to believe someone will do what he promised. It means nothing more.[3] It has nothing to do with obedience and submission. But notice Hodges is not simply letting the word "believe" mean believe. He has added modifiers to the word. He puts it in the context of believing someone will do what he promised. Any language student knows that words are qualified and directed in their meaning by their modifiers. Clearly Hodges is not letting "believe" mean "believe" as he advocates.

Second, we would not argue that we must use the word "believe" without modifiers. The Bible does not do that. But the common modifiers the Bible uses with "believe" do not include Hodges'--that is, saving faith is not simply "to believe Jesus will do what He promised." Rather, the Bible also speaks of believing "in" or "on" the Lord Jesus Christ. Saving faith is believing in a person, which includes His promises but not just His promises.

Third, in another place Hodges' challenge to recognize "believe" and "faith" as equivalents to their Greek counterparts is shown to be incorrect and inconsistent.[4] In discussing the phrase "to save your souls" in James 1:21, he says we must be careful not to define these words according to our modern English. What happened to the theory of the equivalency of English words to their Greek counterparts? What happened to the charge of "an inadequate and misguided view of biblical linguistics"[5] for failing to allow an English word to be equivalent to its Greek counterpart? Or is this principle only applicable when it is helpful to establish one's private opinion?

To summarize:

1. A theory of the complete equivalency of English words to their Greek counterparts is not a sound biblical hermeneutic.

2. To advocate this theory at all is not sound exegesis, but to use it in one place to argue one's position and then to deny it in another place to argue for another of one's convictions is an exegetical inconsistency of grave proportions.

3. To use modifiers with the word "believe" ("believe one will do what he promises") and to seek to define saving faith from the connotation left by the modifiers (which are not Scriptural modifiers) and then talk of wanting to let the word "believe" be equivalent to its Greek counterpart is to stack the exegesis deck in one's favor.

In light of these inconsistencies, the reader can judge who has the "inadequate and misguided view of biblical linguistics."

2. James 2--a Dead Faith

No discussion of the relation of faith and works would be complete without the consideration of James 2:26, which states that "faith without works is dead." In Hodges' handling of the phrase and passage, he says that to conclude that this "dead faith without works" is a false, unsaving faith is "one of the strangest distortions of scripture that has ever occurred."[6] He argues that since James is comparing a "dead faith" to a dead body, we must conclude this faith was once alive.[7] And if it was once alive, then it is still alive. Therefore, since it was once alive and is still alive, it must be a saving faith which is now inactive.

The final conclusion, then, is that James is not speaking of a saving faith versus a false faith which cannot save but rather he is speaking of two kinds of saving faith--an active one and an inactive one. Therefore the presence of works is no proof of salvation, nor is the absence of works the evidence of a lack of salvation. A Christian can be one who has works or one who has no works. Works have nothing to do with salvation. They neither produce it or prove it. "Faith without works is dead" means that such a faith is a saving faith, but it has now become inactive.

Obviously, James is using a metaphor here, comparing a "dead faith" to a dead body. One must be careful in interpreting such an expression not to read more into it than is there. Hodges admits this limitation of metaphors in the discussion of another passage as he speaks of the vine-branch metaphor of John 15.[8] As he interprets the statement that the branches are cut off and burned with fire, he takes these branches as believers. The problem with this interpretation is that the metaphor of being cut off and burned disallows any possible restoration to relationship and fellowship with the branch. It is here that he warns that all illustrations have limits, indicating that we should not push them to their extreme possibilities.[9]

But is that not what Hodges has done in James 2? He says he would conclude two things if he saw a body as he walked down a street: first, that its life-giving spirit is gone, and second, that it was at one time alive.[10] Several problems emerge from such a statement.

First, if its life-giving spirit is gone, it is dead. It is not just inactive--it is a dead body. It has no life! This author speaks with a smile and a twinkle in his eye but he cannot refrain from saying that if Hodges doesn't know the difference between an inactive body and a dead body (one having no life-giving spirit), he surely wouldn't ever want to lie down and go to sleep in Hodges' presence. Hodges might call the undertaker and haul him off to the cemetery. The text speaks of a dead body--one having no life-giving spirit, not just an inactive one.

Hodges would be more consistent in taking an Arminian position than the one he does. The body was alive, but now it is dead, for its life-giving spirit is gone. That is, the person was alive, but is now dead. That is, he was saved but is now lost. That would be consistent.

Hodges should have remembered his warning concerning metaphors in the other passage cited.[11] The metaphor of the dead body stresses one thing--that a faith without works is a dead faith--one that has no life-giving spirit. A faith without works is not an inactive faith; it is a dead, false, unsaving faith. That the interpretation of this phrase does not have to conclude that such a faith was once alive is obvious from Paul's statement that in our lost condition we were <u>dead</u> in trespasses and sins. Does that mean we were at one time spiritually alive, and then at another point again we died and became sinners? Not hardly. It is a metaphor stating one thing--we were without the life-giving Spirit of God in trespasses and sin before we were saved.

In summary, Hodges makes several errors in his interpretation of James 2:26.

1. He presses the metaphor to an extreme when it will help his position, while in another place he disallows such a procedure for another metaphor because doing so would bring an unexplainable difficulty to his interpretation.

2. He admits "dead" means the absence of a life-giving spirit, but then says this absence of a life-giving spirit is not death but merely inactivity.

On the basis of these two exegetical errors he concludes James 2:26 does not teach that a faith without works is a false, unsaving faith. Rather it is a saving but inactive faith. Such an interpretation as the former, he insists is "one of the strangest distortions of Scripture which has ever occurred"[12] Again, we shall allow the reader to conclude which interpretation is a strange distortion of Scripture.

3. Romans 10:9-13--Whosoever shall call on the name of the Lord shall be saved.

When one begins to advocate a new view of salvation and several key doctrines surrounding it, one must reinterpret many passages to make them fit the new system. In fact, that may be a clue that one is facing a new system of thinking--the twisting of Scripture to new and bizarre interpretations that no one else has ever advocated simply for the purpose of making them fit the system. This is not to say that new interpretations are to be rejected because they are new. Their faithfulness to Scripture is the key question. The twisting to fit the system is the primary factor, but their newness is a warning.

This is the case with several passages dealt with by Hodges: passages almost universally understood in the history of the church, totally reinterpreted to agree with his system.

One passage which stands as a clear example of this action is Romans 10:9-13, especially verse 13, the well-known verse which declares, "Whosoever shall call upon the name of the Lord shall be saved." "Calling on the name of the Lord" is declared to be the action of a Christian and not that of a lost person. "Saved" is reinterpreted to speak of the deliverance of a Christian from some problem or danger, rather than of a sinner being delivered from the penalty and power of sin.[13]

If one asks how that can be done in light of the context, which seems to be speaking of salvation, one is told that such is not the case. The whole passage speaks of the saved person, not the lost. Then it becomes clear why the whole section has to be reinterpreted--it speaks of confessing with one's mouth the Lord Jesus (Romans 10:8-9)--something non-lordship salvation cannot allow as a part of salvation, for that would add another condition to salvation besides faith.[14] Thus the "saving" of this passage is the saving of the saved. This expresses "that wonderful flexibility which always marked the Greek words for 'salvation' . . . "[15]

In summary, Hodges' non-lordship view declares concerning Romans 10:8-13:

1. This is not a context of salvation.

2. The word salvation in this context refers to the deliverance of a Christian from troubles, etc., and not a sinner from the penalty or power of sin.

3. The calling on the name of the Lord is the activity of a Christian and not that of a lost sinner.

4. The confession with the mouth the Lord Jesus, and the believing in the heart that God has raised Him from the dead is again the work of a Christian and not of a lost person.

Hodges' whole case rests on whether the context is one of salvation or one which speaks of a Christian. If it can be shown this is a context of salvation, then his definitions concerning "salvation" and "calling on the name of the Lord," etc., are clearly shown to be imaginative creations to fit a system.

Is this a salvation context and passage? The answer is undeniably yes. Note the following:

verse 1
Paul declares that his heart's desire and prayer for Israel is that they may be saved. Does this not speak of a salvation of lost Israel and not a saved Israel? If anyone has any doubt, read verse two.

verse 2
Paul bears a witness that Israel has a zeal for God, but not according to God. Clearly verses 1-2 speak of lost Israel. If anyone still doubts, read on.

verse 3
Paul declares Israel is ignorant of God's righteousness, and therefore they are going about to establish their own righteousness. They refuse to submit themselves to the righteousness of God. Does this not speak of salvation?

verses 4-8
Paul speaks of a righteousness which comes to the one who believes (vs. 4). Paul mentions Moses' description of a righteousness by the law (vs. 5). The righteousness by faith speaks of a word which is near, even in one's mouth and in the heart--it is the word of faith which we preach (vss. 6-8).

Is it not clear that Romans 10:1-8 is a context of salvation? Could it possibly be that verses 9-13 suddenly without any transition or hint of change switch to speak of Christians and not of salvation? Hardly. Consider the continuation of the context of salvation which is clear.

verse 9
Paul declares salvation comes by confessing the Lord Jesus and believing in the heart that God has raised Him from the dead.

verse 10
>   Paul states it is with the heart that man believes unto
>   righteousness, and with the mouth confession is made
>   unto salvation.

verse 11
>   Paul declares that the one believing on Him will never be
>   ashamed.

verses 12-13
>   Paul declares that God hears both Jew and Gentile who
>   call upon Him. Whoever calls on the name of the Lord
>   shall be saved.

verses 14-17
>   Paul reasons in these verses of the need to spread the
>   gospel to all men. Before men can call on the Lord in
>   faith preachers must be sent so they can preach, so men
>   can hear, so men can then be saved. Paul concludes by
>   declaring that faith comes by hearing and hearing by the
>   word of God.

Undeniably the entire context is one of salvation. To be
saved speaks of lost men believing. Salvation speaks of
sinners being delivered from the penalty and power of sin.
To apply several of these verses to Christians calling on the
Lord to be delivered from their trials is to twist the Scriptures
in violation of its obvious context and plain meaning to a
new and bizarre interpretation advocated by no one of this
writer's knowledge simply to fit the system of non-lordship
theology.

4. II Corinthians 13:5--Examine yourselves, whether you are in the faith.

It is not possible to discuss how Hodges handles the
numerous passages of Scripture that relate to the Lordship
controversy. A few key passages have been chosen in order
that the reader might gain a clear understanding of his

dedication to make them compatible to his over-all system even if he must force them in his exegesis.

Another example of this is II Corinthians 13:5 where Paul challenges his readers to examine themselves to determine whether they are in the faith. The word for examine means "to put to the test" or "to prove" whether they are in the faith. The following sentence in the Biblical text declares that there are two possibilities: either Jesus Christ is in them or He is not, which is shown to be the case if they fail the test.

Hodges is convinced these words have been "sadly misconstrued,"[16] and it is not possible that Paul could be challenging his readers to determine if they are or are not saved. Such an interpretation is "unthinkable" because Paul has not questioned their salvation previously in the epistle.[17] Because Paul uses the phrase "in the faith" elsewhere in his writings to speak of believers, the same phrase must be used in II Corinthians 13:5 to speak of believers also.[18] In I Corinthians 16:13 he challenges his readers to "stand fast in the faith." In Romans 14:1 Paul speaks of being "weak in the faith." In Titus 1:13 his expression is "sound in the faith."

Thus in II Corinthians 13:5 it is not a question of whether they are saved or lost, but if they are living a dynamic life of faith or an inactive life of faith. All who are not "in the faith" are "disapproved" by God, but that does not refer to a lost condition.

Hodges' interpretation is questionable in several aspects. He is correct in seeing this as a challenge from Paul for examination of life. That part of the text is undeniable. Somebody in this passage is challenged to examine something. Something is to be "put to the test."

The real issue centers on what is to be examined. That question is answered by the phrase "in the faith." It can hardly be concluded that because Paul uses the phrase "in the faith" in other passages to refer to believers that such is the case here, especially in light of the fact that the phrase is used in the other passages with modifying words. "To stand in the faith" or "to be sound in the faith" obviously speaks of believers. But a challenge to examine oneself whether he is "in the faith" is quite a different matter. To stand in something or to be sound in something is distinct from being in something to begin with.

As for Hodges' contention that this cannot be a challenge to the Corinthians to make certain of their salvation because Paul did no such thing in the first twelve chapters of his epistle--that is a weak and inconclusive argument. Paul may speak to them as true believers in the early part of the epistle, but that would not rule out the possibility of a challenge to be sure of their salvation later in the epistle unless one manufactures some incorrect exegetical or doctrinal presupposition.

A possible explanation (and one is not necessarily needed) would center on the nature of II Corinthians 10-13. Some have felt these chapters are not part of the original epistle of II Corinthians, but were part of a previous letter known as the sorrowful letter or the painful letter, written primarily to put down an opposition party that was discrediting Paul. This writer rejects the dissection of II Corinthians and sees it rather as a whole. Yet there does seem to be a difference between the early part of the epistle and II Corinthians 10-13. Paul is defending his ministry by reluctantly glorying, and there is a contrast here between Paul's life, ministry, and experience and some in the Corinthian church, perhaps even the false teachers who are influencing them.

In light of this different emphasis in chapters 10-13 from the earlier part of the epistle, it should be no surprise if Paul challenges the minority of trouble-makers to be sure they are saved. In fact, there is a possibility and there may be a need for any professing believer whose life is questionable to be challenged to examine the reality of his salvation, unless a preconceived system of theology disallows it.

5. Romans 8:17--Heirs and Joint-heirs with Christ

The usual and straight-forward interpretation of this verse understands Paul is speaking of the privilege of being a child of God. Part of the privilege is to be an heir of God, one who as a joint-heir with Christ receives all the blessings of God bestowed upon the Son of God. And in some manner suffering is related to the reality of being an heir. It is either a proof of our salvation and heirship or it is a result of it. But either way we who are believers are heirs--joint-heirs with God in Christ.

One can see why this verse is a problem for Hodges' system. It appears to state that our suffering with Christ is a proof of our salvation. His definition of saving faith excludes that possibility. Therefore the verse must be reinterpreted.

To accomplish this task he makes the verse speak of two categories of heirs--one to which all believers belong (the heirs), and another reserved for those who go on and serve and suffer for Christ (the joint-heirs).[19] Thus all believers are heirs, but not all believers are joint-heirs because serving and suffering are optional in the Christian life. This elite category of joint-heirs will also receive a "co-glory" with Christ. Here he brings in II Timothy 2:12 as a parallel passage. It speaks of a "co-reigning" with Christ if we suffer with Him. He puts these two together and concludes that co-reigning in the Timothy passage is the same as "co-glorification" in the Romans passage. Thus glorification has become reigning.

The reader should clearly see the exegetical problems in the manner in which Hodges handles this passage. First, his erroneous use of II Timothy 2:12 as a parallel passage is obvious. One speaks of reigning, the other of glorification. The only thing they have in common is suffering, but that is not enough to stretch glorification to mean reigning. On that interpretive principle confusion would reign (pardon the pun) in Scripture. If one verse spoke of justification and sanctification, and another spoke of justification and forgiveness, one could conclude that forgiveness equals sanctification.

The Greek word in Romans 8:17 speaks of glorification and not reigning. It is a word related to the one translated "glorified" in verse 30 of the same chapter. The word in verse 17 is a compound verb (a prepositional prefix with a simple verb), while the word in verse 30 is the simple verb alone. Hodges should have tied these two verses together rather than link verse 17 and its verb with a completely different context and verb. It is not absolutely necessary for two words in the same context to mean the same thing, but it is better hermeneutics to consider the possibility than to link it with a verb which has no relation in context or meaning.

To take the word in its definition of "glorification" is not possible for Hodges. To do so would ruin his "two heirs" interpretation, for the elite group of suffering joint heirs are the ones who are glorified together with Christ. This would rule out glorification for the first category of non-suffering heirs. Obviously Hodges does not wish to teach this, so he must redefine glorification.

Clearly both a simple reading of the passage and a careful interpretation of the passage bring us to the same conclusion. We are heirs--joint-heirs with God in Christ. The reality of our relation to Christ is shown in our lives of suffering for Him, and we shall be glorified together with Him.

6. I Corinthians 6:9-10--Inheriting the Kingdom of God

One of the first verses which might come to mind to establish a relationship between salvation and a godly life would be I Corinthians 6:9-10. In this passage we are told that those who possess certain life-styles will not inherit the kingdom of God.

9 Know ye not that the unrighteous shall not inherit the kingdom of God? Be not deceived: neither fornicators, nor idolaters, nor adulterers, nor effeminate, nor abusers of themselves with mankind,

10 Nor thieves, nor covetous, nor drunkards, nor revilers, nor extortioners, shall inherit the kingdom of God.

How does Hodges deal with this passage in light of his definition of saving faith?

He develops an argument stating that "inheriting the kingdom" is not the same as "entering the kingdom."[20] The kingdom is entered by all believers but it is inherited only by the same elite he developed in his interpretation of Romans 8:17. In order that one may some day own the kingdom, one must persevere. To enter the kingdom one simply believes according to Hodges' definition of faith. Thus one can be a professing Christian and live a continual life-style of fornication, or adultery, or idolatry, or thieving, or drunkenness, or extortion, etc. (see the text), and no one should raise any question about the reality of such a profession. That kind of person with such a profane life-style will enter the kingdom, but he will not inherit it--that is, own it or reign with Christ. Hodges contends that any other interpretation is unfair to the text,[21] "hopelessly confused,"[22] and "extremely careless."[23]

Such strong and accusing words are not a suitable substitute for sound exegesis. Hodges' position has definite weaknesses. For one thing it piggy-backs on his false distinction of two kinds of heirs in Romans 8:17. We have already shown the fallacies of his exegesis there. There are no two categories of believers--one who is joint-heir who owns the kingdom and reigns with Christ and another who simply enters the kingdom as an heir but does not own it nor reign with Christ.

The fact that salvation results in a breaking with sin and a godly walk is established clearly by Paul in verse 11 of I Corinthians 6, which states, "And such were some of you: But you are washed, but you are sanctified, but you are justified in the name of the Lord Jesus, and by the Spirit of God." Paul says that some of you Corinthians were of the various sinful life-styles named in verses 9-10, but now you are washed, sanctified, and justified in the name of the Lord Jesus and by the Spirit of God. They were these things-- that is, they possessed such life-styles before salvation--but not now. The "but" here is the strong adversative in the Greek. It sets off their present life-style against the former life-style. It does not allow Hodges' definition of saving faith which results in no change of life-style. Neither does it allow his attempt to define inheriting the kingdom as a separate category from entering it. Again, we will leave it to the readers to decide whose interpretation is unfair to the text, hopelessly confused, and extremely careless.

CONCLUSION

Six passages which are important in the non-lordship view of salvation have now been discussed. There is no way possible all the key verses could be considered in this chapter. Enough has been said to enlighten the reader regarding the exegetical methodology of the primary advocate of the non-lordship view. With a weak exegetical methodology, the conclusion of the exegesis as well as the total system the exegesis is seeking to establish comes into serious question.

As another author has written,

> Perhaps one of the most intriguing--and disturbing--features of Zane C. Hodges's book [referring to Gospel Under Siege] . . . is that to the best of my knowledge not one significant interpreter of Scripture in the entire history of the church has held to Hodges's interpretation of the passages he treats. That does not necessarily mean Hodges is wrong; but it certainly means that he is probably wrong, and it probably means he has not reflected seriously enough on the array of fallacies connected with distanciation.[24]

It should be noted that Carson's words are spoken of Hodges' interpretation in his early book, The Gospel Under Siege, but the same statement, in this writer's opinion, is true of his larger and latest book on the same subject, Absolutely Free!.

CHAPTER 7

THEOLOGICAL WEAKNESSES

A theological system based on shaky exegesis and containing numerous straw man statements should be suspect to anyone. But such is not always the case. It is hoped the reader has seen the questionable handling of Scripture by Hodges, and some of his statements which are little more than straw men. We now turn to analyze some of his theological commitments. An attempt will be made to be brief so more areas can be discussed.

1. Non-lordship salvation has a faith which is little more than mental assent.

For Hodges faith is "the inward conviction that what God says to us in the gospel is true."[1] In case one might misconstrue his statement thinking it is more than that, he says just following this definition of faith, "that--and that alone--is saving faith."[2] That he is serious in this definition and faithful to it is borne out in his entire book.

In the same above context he shows a disdain for calling his position "intellectual assent."[3] Yet he never explains how his view differs substantially from mental or intellectual assent. His definition does not include the will of man for he actually says that a man can believe against his will.[4] One thing you must say about Hodges--he is consistent to his definition. And certainly if saving faith is no more than an inward conviction of the truth of what God says to us in the gospel, that definition itself rules out anything and everything except mental agreement or intellectual assent. Though Hodges may wish to distance himself from this charge, the more he discusses the issue, the less he dispels

it. How else is one to take a further statement where he
indicates that saving faith is "merely believing facts?"[5]

2. Non-lordship salvation has a new birth that does not necessarily transform.

Hodges never denies the miracle of the new birth. He
acknowledges it is that--a miracle which imparts new life to
the sinner.[6] By it a regenerated sinner possesses God's
Son--He is his life. Also, the believer who has this life will
know it.[7] One cannot possess that life without knowing it.

Yet one can experience this new birth and not be
transformed. The sinner may turn from his sin or he may
not. He may submit to Christ or he may not. He may
follow Christ or he may not. He may live a godly life or he
may not. He may love God and hate sin or he may not. He
may be a disciple or he may not. He may live in the most
despicable life-style of sin or he may not. He may change
the direction of his life or he may not. It is hoped he will
leave sin, follow Christ, and live for Him, but he may not.

Thus non-lordship salvation has a new birth which does
not necessarily transform--it may or it may not. One
wonders what happened to Paul's statement that if anyone be
in Christ, he is a new creature. Old things have passed away
and all things have become new (II Corinthians 5:17).

3. Non-lordship salvation has a discipleship that is optional.

Because Hodges insists that the call to salvation is
separate from the call to discipleship,[8] he is forced to the
tenuous position of an optional discipleship. He pictures
discipleship as an enrollment in a difficult and demanding
school.[9] There is a cost to enrollment, and before one
enrolls he should consider it very carefully. Don't enroll
unless you are desirous to carry it through.

One almost gets the impression it's alright not to be a
disciple--just be as good a Christian as you can. Be a

faithful church member and a nice moral person but discipleship is optional. There's no shame if one concludes the program is too demanding and therefore doesn't enroll. It's nice if you would, but if you can't that's alright too.

Granted, Hodges does not say it is optional, but the chapter on discipleship could lead to that conclusion. If the preacher tells people to wait for anything before they enroll or become disciples, including until they are ready, how does one think they will respond? If one replies that the Holy Spirit will lead them into discipleship, then why can't He accomplish that at salvation? Surely as He regenerates He will transform and grant a desire to follow in the joy and sacrifice of discipleship.

4. Non-lordship salvation has a faith which can exist without any presence of works as a result or evidence.

Because Hodges never understands the true relation of the grace of saving faith and the result of godly works, works are optional as well. He continually sees a disjunction between the two. If anything is said to accompany saving faith, or if anything is said to result from saving faith, in Hodges' mind it must be seen as a condition or means of salvation. He never hints that he has even begun to understand or sought to understand their correct relation, but his logic has established a basic premise which prohibits him from so doing. His basic premise is that any accompaniment or result of saving faith would be a condition or means of salvation. Once established this premise shoots down all accompaniments or results of salvation and leaves saving faith stripped of its power and content, and leaves a salvation without the presence of works as a result or evidence of salvation.

5. Non-lordship salvation has a repentance which has no part in salvation.

To say the least Hodges has a view of repentance which to this writer's knowledge is unlike any view held previously in the history of Christian doctrine. As an initial act it can take place before the salvation experience or following it or perhaps never.[10] The view of historic Christianity is that repentance initially takes place at salvation and yet it should be a central attitude and action of the child of God following his salvation. For Hodges, however, the call to faith has to do with receiving eternal life, while the call to repentance is simply a call to harmony with God and has nothing to do with eternal life.[11] One can even have eternal life without harmony with God (repentance) or one can possess harmony (repentance) with God without having eternal life.

Further, if repentance has to do with harmony with God and with fellowship with God, and if repentance can come some time before salvation (statements all affirmed by Hodges), the conclusion of this logic is unbelievable. It means that one can have harmony and fellowship with God without being saved, that is, without being a child of God. Hodges does not state that conclusion, but it is correct on the basis of the premises he states.

Not all non-lordship salvation advocates define repentance in the same way,[12] but all would in some manner redefine it and either remove it from the time of salvation (Hodges) or remove from it any concept of turning from sin. Again, this is consistent with the non-lordship view of saving faith.

One of Hodges' main arguments for severing repentance and faith in the work of salvation is the gospel of John. Because he does not find the word repentance in John, a book which was written with an evangelistic purpose, he concludes that repentance has no part in salvation.[13] But even this in reality is not enough to settle the issue, for it is obvious according to the other gospels and the rest of the New Testament that Jesus and the apostles preached repentance and faith. Evidently Hodges realizes this and therefore he must still redefine repentance to separate it from salvation.

The argument that repentance is not part of salvation because of its absence in the gospel of John is a weak argument on several counts. Anyone familiar with the gospel of John knows it is a book of contrasts: light versus darkness, truth versus error, belief versus unbelief, life versus death, the believer versus the world, etc. To come to Christ by faith includes the renunciation and removal from one side of the contrast to the embracing and entrance into the other side of the contrast. One renounces the darkness, and embraces and enters His light. One renounces error and embraces the truth. One rejects unbelief, which is based on self and falsehood, and embraces Christ in trust and confidence. One is removed from death and enters the realm of life.

One cannot come to Christ and remain in darkness, for He is the light. One cannot come to Christ and continue to embrace error, for He is truth. One cannot come to Christ and remain in death, for He is life. One cannot come to Christ and continue to cling to unbelief. One cannot come to Christ without renouncing self, the world, darkness, error, falsehood, etc. This is the background and context of John.

For example, in John 6 the contrast is clear. The people following Him are selfish and desirous of a king to deliver them from their oppression. They have no concept of nor desire for His Messianic role. There is a worldly thirst for physical bread, while His is a spiritual message of eating His flesh and drinking His blood. Their unbelief shows an unwillingness to renounce self, sin, the world, darkness, and unbelief so they might embrace Christ in faith. This is a refusal to repent. To come to Christ in faith would have included these elements. Clearly, repentance is found in John in concept though not in the word itself.

As for the redefining of the term "repentance" as done by the non-lordship position, it is sufficient to ask the reader to compare the footnote data and authorities presented in MacArthur as he presents the Lordship position[14] with the Ryrie footnote data[15] and the Hodges authorities[16] for the non-lordship position. MacArthur supports the historic position of repentance by reference to <u>The New International Dictionary of New Testament Theology</u> (Colin Brown,

editor); Vine's Expository Dictionary of Old and New
Testament Words (W. E. Vine); The Theological Dictionary
of the New Testament (Gerhard Kittel, editor); Greek-
English Lexicon of the New Testament (Joseph Henry
Thayer); etc. Does not this weak lexical support for the non-
lordship view raise the possibity of an accusation of a lack of
scholarly research, which in turn leads to the defining of
words based on one's own opinions, which in turn
necessitates straw men to support one's views?

Thus non-lordship salvation has a repentance that has no
part in salvation (according to Hodges), and a definition of
repentance that is not supportable from Scripture, the best
word-study authorities, or the history of Christian doctrine.

6. Non-lordship salvation has a security without perseverance.

Because saving faith is separated from repentance, and
because it has no certain accompaniments or results, non-
lordship salvation has no doctrine of perseverance. One may
continue or he may not. One may persevere or he may not.
Yet at the same time, non-lordship salvation believes
salvation is a free gift and it is forever.[17] Thus one can be
saved and not persevere.

Lordship salvation believes salvation is a free eternal
gift, but also that because it is the work of the Holy Spirit
based on God's eternal purpose that the believer will
persevere (Philippians 1:6). That is, perseverance will be
the overall pattern of the believer's life. This is not to seek
to force or coerce people to live godly lives, but is stated as a
fact based on God's power and purpose in salvation.

The problem with the non-lordship view is that it opens
the door for a "carnal security." If one has exercised faith
(as defined by non-lordship), one could rejoice over the
benefits of salvation, including its eternal character, while
rejecting any further call to spirituality, godliness,
commitment, or service. Every pastor has felt a certain
frustration and burden when facing such a person who
possesses a bold confidence and smiling assurance while

almost laughing at any call or challenge to love and serve Christ. How does one deal with such a person according to non-lordship salvation? How does one practice church discipline from such a foundation, which, though not directly advocating carnal security, still indirectly encourages it? Does not the church today suffer already from a weakened view of salvation which encourages carnal security without another segment of the church contributing further to the problem? What kind of grace is it anyway that is powerful to save from the wrath and penalty of sin but not from the power of sin?

7. Non-lordship salvation has an anti-Calvinistic bias which leaves it with a God who cannot accomplish His purpose in salvation.

Lordship salvation flows from a Calvinistic foundation. God has chosen a people and He will save them. He regenerates them and grants them the gifts of repentance and faith. Such a work of salvation transforms them. God has also justified them and He has begun the work of sanctification in them which He will also perfect. Through trials, difficulties, and even failures, they are not only eternally secure but will persevere in holiness and faith.

Hodges' view, however, possesses an anti-Calvinistic bias. Though he does speak of God's sovereignty in salvation, and of the necessity of emphasizing human responsibility[18] (with which Calvinism would agree), he tips the scale in the transaction of salvation toward man.[19] Though salvation is a free eternal gift by the power of the Holy Spirit, the final determination to serve and persevere is in the hands of man. God's power in sanctification and perseverance is weak and incapable of completing the work without the power of man.

His anti-Calvinistic bias comes through strongly several times as he ties Lordship salvation into hyper-Calvinistic viewpoints without one shred of documentation. He says in one place,

> Frequently (though not always) lordship salvation is combined
> with a harsh system of thought that denies the reality of God's
> love for every single human being. According to this kind of
> theology God dooms most men to eternal damnation long before
> they are born and really gives His Son to die only for the elect.[20]

Here he mixes the hyper-Calvinist doctrine of a limited
love of God for men with a caustic undefined form of
reprobation and with a limited atonement (held by all five-
point Calvinists). He ties all of it in with Lordship salvation.
He is kind enough to admit that not all Lordship people
believe this, but where is his documentation for this
statement? He says this is done frequently, so he should be
able to document ample Lordship people who adhere to all
these views in his strange mixture.

The truth of the matter is that he has built another straw
man by including these three theological concepts as one and
by inserting them in his argumentation when they really are
not needed. Is he not hoping to help his non-lordship view
by belittling another view by false association?

He states again in the same context,

> No system of thought which reduces human beings to mere
> robots, or to a collection of puppets on strings does justice
> to the Bible's deep insistence on human responsibility.[21]

Again one wonders why this is inserted and what it adds
to his argument. And is he so uninformed theologically that
he really believes this is a fair and accurate description of
Calvinism and Lordship salvation? He does the same thing
in another context,[22] mentioning limited atonement again
almost as part and parcel of Lordship salvation. This is not
to deny that limited atonement is part of Calvinism, at least
five-point Calvinism. It is to question Hodges' insertion of
that as an issue into the Lordship debate in a context where it
is unnecessary, and to make such statements without
documentation.

It is true that Lordship salvation flows from a Calvinistic
basis, but Hodges has failed to prove that anyone who holds
to Lordship salvation agrees with Calvinism as he defines it

above, let alone that the two (his incorrect definition of Calvinism and Lordship salvation) are associated "frequently." He also fails to show the clear relation between his statements on Calvinism and the subject he is discussing in the two contexts. His anti-Calvinistic bias is shown in the presentation of his own view and in his misrepresentations of the Lordship view.

8. Non-lordship salvation is grounded upon an extreme dispensationalism.

The Lordship debate is not a controversy between dispensationalists and non-dispensationalists. Interestingly, the two major proponents of each side, John MacArthur and Zane Hodges, are both dispensationalists. Even dispensationalists disagree concerning the relation of law and grace, which is a central question in the Lordship controversy.

Many early dispensationalists held an antithetical view of law and grace. The Old Testament was the period of the law, and the New Testament is the period of grace. Never can or shall the two be mixed. This was the view of Lewis Sperry Chafer, the original Scofield Bible, and other early dispensationalists.[23] Such a conviction led early dispensationalists to deny that certain portions of Scriptures, even New Testament portions, are for us today, such as the Sermon on the Mount by Christ.[24]

In the passing of the years dispensationalism, like all theological systems, was called upon to defend itself, especially its supposed extremes. The result of this theological give-and-take was an evolution and modification of the position. Many dispensationalists came to see the indefensibility of an antitheses and exclusiveness between law and grace. These men never left dispensationalism, with its structuring of God's plan in dealing with mankind into dispensations, nor the distinctive relation of Israel and the Church, but they did hear the criticism and recognized the problem of the early extremes of dispensationalism.

On the other hand, some dispensationalists have continued to hold to the early extremes, and thus still argue for a concept of salvation based on an antithesis and exclusiveness of law and grace. Thus the Hodges view of a salvation without repentance or works as an evidence or result of salvation is convinced it is defending this necessary distinction between law and grace even today.[25] His commitment to the antithetical and exclusive nature of law and grace is so strong that he must redefine historic Christian doctrine (faith, repentance, etc., as we have seen), and he must reinterpret clear Scriptural passages, even twisting them to make them fit his basic erroneous premise.

The reader should understand that one does not have to follow Hodges if he is a dispensationalist. Some dispensationalists, including John MacArthur, have repudiated Hodges' position. It is hoped that others will follow.

SUMMARY AND CONCLUSION

So that the reader may see these theological weaknesses as a whole, and so the reader may understand their seriousness, they are as follows.

1. Non-lordship salvation has a faith which is little more than mental assent.

2. Non-lordship salvation has a new birth that does not necessarily transform.

3. Non-lordship salvation has a discipleship that is optional.

4. Non-lordship salvation has a faith which can exist without any presence of works as a result or evidence.

5. Non-lordship salvation has a repentance which has no part in salvation.

6. Non-lordship salvation has a security without perseverance.

7. Non-lordship salvation has an anti-Calvinistic bias which leaves it with a God who cannot accomplish His purpose in salvation.

8. Non-lordship salvation is grounded upon an extreme dispensationalism.

CONCLUSION

It appears that our task is almost finished. Both positions of the Lordship controversy have been presented. They have been compared by noting major areas of their theological differences, and by presenting their interpretations of key Scripture passages. Finally, three chapters of critique have been set forth concerning the weaknesses of the non-lordship view. Several observations will finish our task.

First, the reader by now should understand that the Lordship debate is not just a matter of semantics. That is, it is not just a debate of words. It is not the nit-picking of theologians and Bible scholars brought about by their slicing of subjects and passages thinner than the layman could care or understand. It does not concern unimportant issues which make no difference in the evangelical world. Rather the debate concerns major theological doctrines with the two views taking opposite positions which will have an influence practically on the church for years to come. Clearly the debate should not be minimized. Both Hodges and MacArthur are correct--the debate concerns the very nature of the gospel. That being the case, it is important for Christians to be informed and come to the proper conclusions on the matter. The debate is not likely to go away soon, nor is it expected to cool down any time soon either.

Second, this writer in no way would encourage the reader to limit his or her pursuit of the subject to this book alone. It is hoped that interest in the debate has been stirred and information has been imparted in the subject areas and key passages. May the reader continue to study the issues of the debate, including the reading of the Hodges and the MacArthur books. Most of all, may the reader search the Word of God, for it alone is our authority.

Third, this writer wants to go on record that though he is in strong agreement with MacArthur in the basic tenets of his book, that does not necessarily mean he agrees with every statement MacArthur makes or level of emphasis he gives each issue in his book. Writing a book itself is a debatable task. Decisions have to be made concerning the subjects, the organization of subjects, words to convey the concepts, the critique of the subjects, etc. Many times an author himself sees things he would have done differently were he to write the book again. This is not to denegrate the MacArthur book in any way. It is a valuable and well-written and challenging book, but certainly not infallible.

There is a sense in which one can understand a subject, its importance, or the emphasis an author gives areas of it only by knowing the context out of which a work is written. Therefore, if some of the statements of the MacArthur book seem strong, they will be better understood after reading the non-lordship writers. The same is no doubt true of the non-lordship writers' statements. It would be hoped that strong statements from both sides of the controversy would be in fairness, absent of any caustic spirit, and reserved for the theological issues and not for persons.

After all is said and done, we can surely trust the Lord of the church to guide his people into the truth and to establish them in it. Yet at the same time we must be diligent to study the issues, search the Scriptures, pray for His guidance, and then having understood the truth, to stand faithfully for it, especially in an area or time when the very nature of the gospel itself is at stake.

ENDNOTES

INTRODUCTION

[1] Lewis Sperry Chafer, Grace (Findlay, Ohio: Dunham Publishing Company, 1922), pp. 16-19.

[2] Charles C. Ryrie, Balancing the Christian Life (Chicago: Moody Press, 1969), pp. 169-181.

[3] See especially Zane Hodges, The Gospel Under Siege (Dallas, TX: Redencion Viva, 1981).

[4] John MacArthur, The Gospel According to Jesus (Grand Rapids, MI: Zondervan Publishing Co., 1988).

[5] Zane Hodges, Absolutely Free! (Dallas, TX: Redencion Viva, 1989), and Charles C. Ryrie, So Great Salvation, (Wheaton, IL: Victor Books, 1989).

[6] Hodges, Absolutely Free!, p. 19.

[7] Ibid., p. 20.

[8] Ibid., p. 25.

[9] Ibid., p. 26.

[10] Ibid., p. 27.

[11] Ibid.

[12] Ibid.

[13] Ibid.

[14] Ibid., p. 31.

[15]Ibid., p. 48.

[16]Ibid., p. 49.

[17]Ibid., p. 135.

[18]Ibid., p. 148.

[19]Ibid., p. 169.

[20]Ibid., p. 183.

[21]Hodges, Gospel under Siege, pp. 6 and 122.

[22]Ibid., p. 121.

[23]Ibid., p. 97.

[24]Ibid., p. 10.

[25]MacArthur, p. ix.

[26]Ibid., pp. ix and xi.

[27]Ibid., p. ix.

[28]Ibid.

[29]Ibid., p. xi.

[30]Ibid.

[31]Ibid.

[32]Ibid., p. xii.

[33]Ibid., p. xiv.

[34]Ibid.

[35] Ibid., p. 15.

[36] Ibid.

[37] Ibid., p. 16.

[38] Ibid.

[39] Ibid.

[40] Ibid., p. 17.

[41] Ibid., p. 22.

[42] Ibid., p. 30.

CHAPTER ONE

[1] Hodges, <u>Absolutely Free!</u>.

[2] Ibid., pp. 26-29.

[3] Ibid., pp. 29-32.

[4] Ibid., p. 31.

[5] Ibid., pp. 37-43.

[6] Ibid., p. 47.

[7] Ibid., p. 49.

[8] Ibid., p. 50.

[9] Ibid.

[10] Ibid., p. 51.

[11] Ibid., p. 52.

[12]Ibid.

[13]Ibid., p. 55.

[14]Ibid., p. 56.

[15]Ibid., p. 57.

[16]Ibid., p. 59.

[17]Ibid., p. 63.

[18]Ibid., pp. 67-76.

[19]Ibid., p. 68.

[20]Ibid.

[21]Ibid., p. 69.

[22]Ibid., p. 70.

[23]Ibid., pp. 70 and 93.

[24]Ibid., p. 74.

[25]Ibid., p. 79.

[26]Ibid., p. 80.

[27]Ibid.

[28]Ibid., pp. 81-82.

[29]Ibid., pp. 83-84.

[30]Ibid., p. 83.

[31]Ibid., p. 84.

[32]Ibid., p. 85.

[33]Ibid., p. 86.

[34]Ibid., p. 87.

[35]Hodges, <u>Gospel under Siege</u>, pp. 70-71.

[36]Ibid., pp. 72-73.

[37]Hodges, <u>Absolutely Free!</u>, p. 91.

[38]Ibid., p. 92.

[39]Ibid.

[40]Ibid., p. 93.

[41]Ibid.

[42]Ibid.

[43]Ibid., p. 94.

[44]Ibid.

[45]Ibid., p. 95.

[46]Ibid., p. 98.

[47]Ibid., p. 99.

[48]Ibid., p. 117.

[49]Ibid., p. 118.

[50]Ibid.

[51]Ibid., pp. 119-120.

[52]Ibid., pp. 122ff.

[53]Ibid., p. 125.

[54]Ibid.

[55]Ibid.

[56]Ibid., p. 126.

[57]Ibid., p. 130.

[58]Ibid., pp. 130-131.

[59]Ibid., p. 131.

[60]Ibid., p. 132.

[61]Ibid., p. 133.

[62]Ibid.

[63]Ibid., p. 135.

[64]Ibid., pp. 136-137.

[65]Ibid.

[66]Ibid., p. 137.

[67]Ibid., p. 138.

[68]Ibid., p. 140.

[69]Ibid., p. 144.

[70]Ibid.

[71]Ibid., p. 145.

72Ibid.

73Ibid.

74Ibid., p. 146.

75Ibid., pp. 146f.

76Ibid., pp. 149-150.

77Ibid., p. 151.

78Ibid.

79Ibid., pp. 156-157.

80Ibid., p. 159.

81Ibid., p. 168.

82Ibid., p. 169.

83Ibid.

84Ibid., pp. 169-170.

85Ibid., p. 169.

86Ibid., p. 172.

87Ibid., p. 173.

88Ibid., pp. 181f.

89Ibid., p. 181.

90Ibid., p. 182.

91Ibid., p. 183.

[92]Ibid., p. 183f.

CHAPTER TWO

[1]MacArthur, <u>Gospel According to Jesus</u>, p. 21.

[2]Ibid.

[3]Ibid.

[4]Ibid., p. 22.

[5]Ibid., pp. 22-23.

[6]Ibid., p. 28.

[7]Ibid., p. 31.

[8]Ibid., p. 32.

[9]Ibid., p. 37.

[10]Ibid., p. 38.

[11]Ibid., p. 44.

[12]Ibid., pp. 48f.

[13]Hodges, <u>Absolutely Free!</u>, pp. 157-158.

[14]Ibid., pp. 49-50.

[15]MacArthur, p. 52.

[16]Ibid., pp. 55f.

[17]Ibid., p. 56.

[18]Ibid.

19Ibid., p. 58.

20Ibid., p. 59.

21Ibid., p. 60.

22Ibid., pp. 61, 65.

23Ibid., p. 65.

24Ibid., p. 67.

25Ibid.

26Ibid., p. 75.

27Ibid.

28Ibid., p. 77.

29Ibid., pp. 77-88.

30Ibid., pp. 91f.

31Ibid., p. 95.

32Ibid., pp. 97f.

33Ibid., p. 107.

34Ibid., p. 108.

35Ibid., p. 109.

36Ibid., p. 110.

37Ibid., p. 111.

38Ibid., p. 112.

[39]Ibid.

[40]Ibid., p. 113.

[41]Ibid., pp. 117f.

[42]Ibid., p. 121.

[43]Ibid., p. 122.

[44]Ibid., p. 123.

[45]Ibid., p. 124.

[46]Ibid., pp. 125-126.

[47]Ibid., p. 127.

[48]Ibid., pp. 128f.

[49]Ibid., p. 130.

[50]Ibid., p. 131.

[51]Ibid.

[52]Ibid., pp. 134f.

[53]Ibid., p. 135.

[54]Ibid., pp. 137-138.

[55]Ibid., p. 135.

[56]Ibid., pp. 139-140.

[57]Ibid., p. 140.

[58]Ibid., p. 141.

[59]Ibid., p. 142.

[60]Ibid., pp. 143f.

[61]Ibid., p. 145.

[62]Ibid., pp. 146f.

[63]Ibid., pp. 150f.

[64]Ibid.

[65]Ibid., p. 151.

[66]Ibid., pp. 152f.

[67]Ibid., pp. 153f.

[68]Ibid., p. 154.

[69]Ibid., p. 159.

[70]Ibid., pp. 160f.

[71]Ibid., pp. 162f.

[72]Ibid., p. 162, referencing Vine.

[73]Ibid., referencing Kittel.

[74]Ibid., pp. 162-163.

[75]Ibid., p. 163.

[76]Ibid., pp. 163-164.

[77]Ibid., p. 165.

[78]Ibid., p. 169.

[79]Ibid., pp. 169f.

[80]Ibid., p. 172.

[81]Ibid., p. 173.

[82]Ibid., pp. 173-174.

[83]Ibid., p. 174.

[84]Ibid., p. 175.

[85]Ibid., p. 176.

[86]Ibid., p. 179.

[87]Ibid., pp. 180ff.

[88]Ibid., pp. 182f.

[89]Ibid., p. 183.

[90]Ibid., pp. 187f.

[91]Ibid., pp. 189f.

[92]Ibid., p. 190.

[93]Ibid., pp. 192f.

[94]Ibid., p. 195.

[95]Ibid., p. 196.

[96]Ibid.

[97]Ibid.

[98]Ibid., p. 197.

[99]Ibid., pp. 198f.

[100]Ibid., pp. 201f.

[101]Ibid., p. 203.

[102]Ibid.

[103]Ibid., pp. 203f.

[104]Ibid., p. 204.

[105]Ibid.

[106]Ibid., p. 205.

[107]Ibid., p. 207.

[108]Ibid., pp. 207-208.

[109]Ibid., pp. 206f.

[110]Ibid., p. 207.

[111]Ibid., p. 209.

[112]Ibid.

[113]Ibid., pp. 213ff.

[114]Ibid.

[115]Ibid., pp. 221ff.

CHAPTER FIVE

[1]Hodges, Absolutely Free!, p. 20.

[2]Ibid., p. 119.

[3]Ibid., pp. 29ff.

[4]Ibid., pp. 47ff.

[5]Ibid., pp. 117f.

[6]Ibid., pp, 92f, The Gospel under Siege, pp. 67f.

[7]Hodges, pp. 93f.

[8]Ibid., pp. 103-104.

[9]Ibid., p. 118.

CHAPTER SIX

[1]Hodges, Absolutely Free!, pp. 29-30.

[2]Ibid.

[3]Ibid., pp. 27-28.

[4]Ibid., p. 120.

[5]Ibid., p. 29.

[6]Ibid., p. 125.

[7]Ibid., p. 126.

[8]Ibid., p. 138.

[9]Ibid.

[10]Ibid., p. 125.

[11]Ibid., p. 138.

[12]Ibid., p. 125.

[13]Ibid., pp. 195f.

[14]Ibid., p. 197.

[15]Ibid., p. 198.

[16]Ibid., p. 200.

[17]Ibid.

[18]Ibid., p. 201.

[19]Hodges, <u>Gospel Under Siege</u>, pp. 109f.

[20]Ibid., pp. 114f.

[21]Ibid., p. 114.

[22]Ibid., p. 115.

[23]Ibid., p. 116.

[24]D.A. Carson, <u>Exegetical Fallacies</u>, (Grand Rapids, MI: Baker Book House, 1984), p. 137.

CHAPTER SEVEN

[1]Hodges, <u>Absolutely Free!</u>, p. 31.

[2]Ibid.

[3]Ibid., p. 30.

[4]Ibid., p. 31.

[5]Ibid., p. 37.

[6]Ibid., p. 49.

[7]Ibid., p. 52.

[8]Ibid., pp. 67f.

[9]Ibid., pp. 75-76.

[10]Ibid., pp. 143f.

[11]Ibid., p. 145.

[12]Charles Ryrie, So Great Salvation, pp. 92-99.

[13]Hodges, Absolutely Free!, p. 147.

[14]MacArthur, pp. 162-163.

[15]Ryrie, So Great Salvation, pp. 92-99.

[16]Hodges, Absolutely Free!, pp. 222-226.

[17]Ibid., p. 59.

[18]Ibid., p. 73. Hodges refers to what God desires and what He decrees. They are not the same, but he never explains God's decrees and their relation to salvation. On the other hand MacArthur in his book refers to and stresses several times the place of God's sovereignty in salvation. See pp. 67-76, 92, 107-111, 146, 172-173.

[19]Ibid., p. 86.

[20]Ibid., pp. 85-86.

[21]Ibid., p. 86.

[22]Ibid., pp. 118-119.

[23]Lewis Sperry Chafer, Grace, pp. 16-19, and C. I. Scofield, The Scofield Reference Bible (New York: Oxford University Press, 1917), p. 1115.

[24]Lewis Sperry Chafer, Systematic Theology, 13th edition, vol. V (Dallas, TX: Dallas Seminary Press, 1948), pp. 97-114. See especially pp. 99 and 113.

[25]Hodges, Absolutely Free!, p. 95. In discussing Lordship salvation's motivation to godly living, Hodges evidences his dispensational leanings. He believes (falsely so) that the motivation to godly living employed by Lordship salvation is the law ("all the thunderings and lightnings from Mt. Sinai"). He cannot see that grace has a proper place for the law in the believer's life.